Main

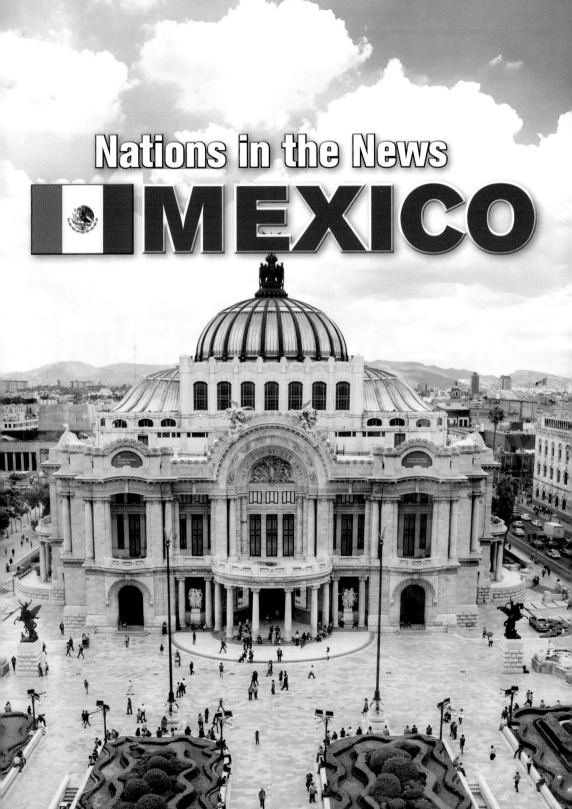

Nations in the News

MEXICO

Afghanistan
China
India
Iran
The Koreas
Mexico
Russia
Saudi Arabia
Syria
United Kingdom

Nations in the News
MEXICO

BY Jennifer L. Rowan

MASON CREST
Philadelphia · Miami

Mason Crest
450 Parkway Drive, Suite D
Broomall, PA 19008
(866) MCP-BOOK (toll free)
www.masoncrest.com

Printed in the United States of America.

First printing
9 8 7 6 5 4 3 2 1

Series ISBN: 978-1-4222-4242-1
Hardcover ISBN: 978-1-4222-4248-3
ebook ISBN: 978-1-4222-7576-4

Cataloging-in-Publication Data is available on file
at the Library of Congress.

Developed and Produced by Print Matters Productions, Inc.
(www.printmattersinc.com)

Cover and Interior Design by Tom Carling, Carling Design Inc.

Contents

KEY ICONS TO LOOK FOR

 Words to Understand: These words with their easy-to-understand definitions will increase the reader's understanding of the text while building vocabulary skills.

 Sidebars: This boxed material within the main text allows readers to build knowledge, gain insights, explore possibilities, and broaden their perspectives by weaving together additional information to provide realistic and holistic perspectives.

 Educational Videos: Readers can view videos by scanning our QR codes, providing them with additional educational content to supplement the text.

 Text-Dependent Questions: These questions send the reader back to the text for more careful attention to the evidence presented there.

 Research Projects: Readers are pointed toward areas of further inquiry connected to each chapter. Suggestions are provided for projects that encourage deeper research and analysis.

 Series Glossary of Key Terms: This back-of-the-book glossary contains terminology used throughout this series. Words found here increase the reader's ability to read and comprehend higher-level books and articles in this field.

The Basilica of Our Lady of Guadalupe is a Roman Catholic church and national shrine in Mexico City.

Mexico at a Glance

Total Land Area	758,449 square miles
Climate	Varies from tropical to desert
Natural Resources	Petroleum, silver, copper, gold, lead, zinc, natural gas, timber
Land Use	Agricultural land: 54.9 percent (11.8 percent arable land, 1.4 percent permanent crops, 41.7 percent permanent pasture); forest: 33.3 percent; other usage: 11.8 percent
Urban Population	80.2 percent of total population (2018)
Major Urban Areas	Mexico City (21.581 million); Guadalajara (5.023 million); Monterrey (4.712 million); Puebla (3.097 million); Toluca de Lerdo (2.354 million); Tijuana (2.058 million)
Geography	North America, south of the United States and north of Belize and Guatemala; maritime borders include the Caribbean Sea and Gulf of Mexico on the eastern coast and the North Pacific Ocean on the west coast; topography includes rugged mountains, high plateaus, low coastal plains, and desert regions

Introduction

The third-largest country in North America, Mexico stretches from the southwestern border of the United States in the north to the borders of Guatemala and Belize in the south, with coastlines on the Pacific Ocean, Caribbean Sea, and Gulf of Mexico. The numerous latitudes of this major Latin American nation create climate zones that vary from deserts in the north to tropical rain forests in the south. Low coastal plains rise quickly inland to the Mexican **Plateau**, and the central part of the country holds the rugged terrain of the Sierra Madres.

Mexico's history has been one of conquest, revolution, development, and conflict. The many iterations of government, coupled with various periods of social and political upheaval, have allowed for the development of corruption in multiple national institutions. Social mobility and economic opportunities are inequitably distributed, and Mexico experiences a high level of poverty, almost 50 percent nationwide.

Pre-Columbian Mexico and European Conquest

Mexico has seen the rise and fall of empires since before the first Europeans stepped foot in what is now the state of Veracruz. Vast **Amerindian** empires controlled the land, often vying against each other for domination. Advanced Mexican civilizations began with the Olmecs, which gave way

Words to Understand

Amerindian: A term for an American Indian, one of the native peoples to inhabit the continents of the Americas prior to European conquest.

Conquistador: A Spanish conqueror in the sixteenth century, specifically of Mexico and Peru.

Indigenous: Referring to the native peoples of a region.

North American Free Trade Agreement (NAFTA): A free trade agreement between Mexico, the United States, and Canada, enacted in 1994 and designed to remove various economic barriers between the three nations.

Plateau: A geographic area of relatively high ground, typically found between mountain ranges or between a lower plains region and a mountain range.

The Mexican landscape varies by region. The Misol Há waterfall can be found in southern Mexico in the municipality of Salto de Agua, whereas the Sonoran Desert lies further north near the U.S.-Mexico border.

to the ancient Maya, Toltec, Zapotec, and Mixtec, and then a new empire of the Maya. These civilizations made advances in science and agriculture, building huge cities that can still be found in ruins today, sometimes deep within Mexico's tropical rain forests.

The last Amerindian civilization to control Mexico was the Aztecs, who lived and ruled their empire from the city of Tenochtitlan, which is now Mexico City. When Spanish **conquistadors** first attempted to land on the coast of the Yucatán peninsula in 1517, the Aztecs drove them off. A second Spanish expedition resulted in the exchange of gifts with the Aztecs. But the third expedition, led by Hernando Cortés in 1519, would become a permanent Spanish conquest. Cortés founded the city of Veracruz and, within three years, defeated the might of the Aztec empire, thanks to advanced European weaponry and the assistance of Amerindian rivals to Aztec power. Tenochtitlan fell to Cortés in 1521, and the rest of Mexico soon followed.

New Spain and Mexican Independence

The Spanish colonial period lasted for 300 years after the conquest of Mexico by Cortés. Spanish holdings stretched from what is now Colorado, Utah, Nevada, and California in the United States, all the way down into South

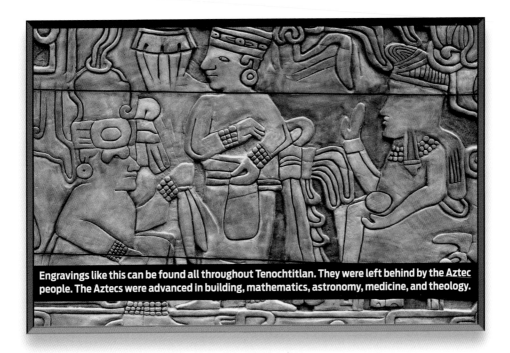

Engravings like this can be found all throughout Tenochtitlan. They were left behind by the Aztec people. The Aztecs were advanced in building, mathematics, astronomy, medicine, and theology.

America. The northern portion, encompassing the American Southwest, Mexico, and Central America, became the Viceroyalty of New Spain.

Wealth from New Spain came from silver and agriculture. A system of trade developed across the Atlantic and was referred to as the Columbian Exchange because it generally followed the routes of Columbus's voyages of discovery. New crops, animals, and precious gems and metals made their way back to Europe from New Spain, whereas the Spaniards introduced European crops, livestock, and deadly diseases like smallpox. These diseases decimated the Amerindian populations of the Americas, including Mexico, leaving only a small percentage of **indigenous** peoples behind. Faced with a shortage of forced labor, it would not be long before the Spanish exploited a third leg of the Columbian Exchange that had developed: bringing captured African slaves to the New World to work the silver mines and growing plantations of cash crops.

A rigid social hierarchy developed in New Spain. At the top were Spanish-born officials, who held all government power and most of the land and wealth. Below them were a group referred to as Creoles— Mexican-born members of society with direct Spanish ancestry. Creoles were often wealthy but generally could not hold government office; many served as military officers. Mestizos, a social group comprising mixed-race individuals with both Spanish and Amerindian ancestry, acted as something of a working middle class. They held roles as shopkeepers, artisans, parish priests, or foot soldiers but generally did not own land and had no voice in government. Full-blooded Amerindians existed below mestizos and were forced to labor in mines or on large estates. The only group below them were African slaves.

Dissatisfaction with this social hierarchy fostered an uprising of mestizos, led by the Catholic priest Miguel Hidalgo y Costilla, known as Father Hidalgo. In 1810, he called upon his parishioners to revolt against oppressive Spanish rule. Unfortunately, he was killed early in the fight for independence. One of his students, José María Morelos y Paván, assumed leadership and, in 1813, established a Congress that formally declared independence from Spain and drafted Mexico's first Constitution. Morelos was captured and executed in 1815, and from there Vincente Guerrero took over.

However, only after the Creole population, motivated by the possibility of governmental power, joined in the movement for independence did the tide begin to turn. A royalist officer named Augustín Iturbide switched sides after Guerrero's defeat and achieved victory over Spain. The 1821 Treaty of Córdoba forced Spain to acknowledge Mexico's independence.

The Mexican Republic

With no government to speak of, Iturbide declared himself emperor in 1822. Guerrero and an army officer named Antonio López de Santa Anna joined forces in opposition, overthrowing Iturbide in 1824. The first Mexican

Statues of Father Hidalgo can be found throughout Mexico. This statue is found outside of Our Lady of Sorrows Parish Church. This is where Father Hidalgo summoned people to listen to his "grito" (or "cry") for independence in 1810.

republic formed under constitutional rule; Gucrrero went on to serve as the republic's second president.

Even at this early stage of democracy, political conflict sprang up between conservative and liberal groups, weakening and dividing the young country. Conservatives, mostly Creoles, wished for a strong central government and the maintenance of traditional privileges. Meanwhile, liberals wanted decentralization of the government, less influence from the Catholic Church, and social reforms intended to promote more equality among free peoples. As in most democratic republics around the world, this tug-of-war between liberals and conservatives persists to this day, shaping modern politics.

Santa Anna assumed the presidency in 1833 and remained in power for over 20 years. Political turmoil and foreign wars depleted Mexico's economic resources and military strength during this time. Some conflicts, such as the war for the independence of Texas in 1836 and the Mexican War with the United States from 1846 to 1848, vastly reduced the size of Mexico's territory. Santa Anna was exiled in 1855, and the liberal Zapotec leader, Benito Juárez, took over.

Juárez worked to reframe the Constitution in 1857, limiting the power of the army and the Catholic Church. The new Constitution also recognized civil marriages and called for a number of freedoms for citizens, including freedom of speech, assembly, and the press. Conservatives opposed the new Constitution, and a three-year civil war bankrupted Mexico and forced Juárez to stop repaying debts owed to France, Britain, and Spain in 1861.

All three European countries subsequently sent troops to Mexico. Britain and Spain withdrew their forces soon after, but French troops remained. France's emperor, Napoleon III, took the opportunity to establish a French monarchy in Mexico, ordering an invasion in 1862. The French were defeated at the Battle of Puebla on May 5, 1862, but the Mexican army, despite being bolstered by this early victory, could not hold off the French. Mexico City was captured, and Mexican forces scattered, resorting to guerilla warfare against the French.

The monarch put on the throne of Mexico, Archduke Maximilian of Austria, tried to rule with benevolence but proved weak. The United States pressured Napoleon III to withdraw troops from Mexico in 1866, leaving Maximilian to fend for himself. He was captured and executed by Mexican republican forces in 1867.

Juárez resumed his role as president of the Mexican republic and immediately set to work improving the country's infrastructure and establishing the foundations of industry. He also introduced public education institutions, providing access to education for many mestizos and Amerindians.

President Benito Juárez.

The Mexican Revolution

Juárez died in 1872, and four years later, one of his generals seized power. Porfirio Díaz ruled Mexico with an iron fist for almost 35 years. Though he stabilized the country, increased agricultural output, and built harbors and railroads, the improvements came with the price of political suppression. Díaz also re-established the privileges of the church, army, and old aristocracy, leading many of Mexico's indigenous peoples and working class to become impoverished. This would prove to be a condition that, for generations up through the current day, these groups would never be able to escape.

The staggering problem of Mexican poverty.

For many in Mexico, Díaz's improvements to the oil industry and infrastructure could not offset the suppression of civil rights and liberties. In 1910, a former bandit and guerilla leader named Pancho Villa led an uprising in the northern part of Mexico, and the cause of landless Amerindians became the crusade of peasant leader Emiliano Zapata. Díaz was forced to resign, and Francisco Madero, a liberal and champion of reform, was elected president in 1911.

Mexico's revolution lasted for seven turbulent years as rival revolutionary leaders engaged in almost constant fighting and violence. Conservative general Victoriano Huerta engineered Madero's assassination in 1913 and took power for himself. Villa and Zapata again rebelled, deposing Huerta, and Venustiano Carranza became president in 1914. But Carranza also faced conflict with Villa and Zapata, prompting U.S. President Woodrow Wilson to intervene twice to attempt to capture Pancho Villa. In 1916, Carranza finally achieved victory and called for a constitutional convention.

The 1917 Constitution harked back to the reforms of Benito Juárez, establishing free public education, regulating hours and wages for workers,

Pancho Villa.

and upholding workers' rights to organize into unions. The Constitution also established the right of the government to reclaim ownership of all land and its resources in the name of the Mexican nation. Many provisions could not be carried out, however, due to a lack of funds and political interest.

The Twentieth Century through Today

Following Carranza's deposition in 1920, subsequent presidents Alvaro Obregán and Plutarco Calles implemented reforms in land distribution, education, and labor. But the pace of reform grew slow under Calles, and between 1928 and 1934, Mexico saw three different presidents take office. The political system fragmented, and in response, Calles established a new political party, the National Revolutionary Party, which would eventually become the Institutional Revolutionary Party (PRI) and Mexico's dominant political party into the twentieth century.

Leaders from the PRI held the presidency until the 1998 presidential election, and they shaped not only Mexico's political system but also its industrialization. They focused on industrial development rather than social or economic reforms, resulting in rapid industrialization and urbanization as people migrated from rural areas to cities in search of work. The population also grew rapidly, prompting the launch of a national family-planning program to stabilize and control population growth.

The discovery of new oil reserves in the late 1970s and early 1980s brought the beginning of economic prosperity, but wasteful spending and ineffective government programs, alongside falling oil prices in 1982, caused the economy to falter. Concerns for Mexico's economic health and growth led to the signing of the **North American Free Trade Agreement (NAFTA)** with the United States and Canada, which helped stabilize Mexico's economy and set the stage for further industrialization and growth.

Alongside economic growth, however, came the continued struggle of many Mexican people living in poverty with little chance for upward social or economic mobility. Overcrowding in cities led to the development of shantytowns, and rural areas increasingly saw government support and welfare programs cut. Making matters worse, political unrest in the 1960s through the 1990s brought guerilla-like activities from various organizations seeking to bring down the established governing party. Soon, political opposition groups sprang up, and the government used both overt and covert force to try to end dissention. During this time, Mexico's crime rate soared as drug cartels grew in size and power in response to growing international demands for the illicit drugs produced and trafficked through Mexico.

Three young girls play barefoot in a poor district of Mexico.

Today, Mexico faces a number of struggles alongside its successes. Reforms in education and health care are slowly improving the lot of many of the neediest Mexicans. But social mobility still lags behind that of similar nations, despite economic growth and diversification of industry. Poverty levels remain high, many Mexicans are directly or indirectly affected by the violence of drug turf wars, and corruption is rampant in certain areas of politics and justice. Further, tensions with the United States over border security have captured global attention as the two countries engage in a struggle over who will control the flow of illicit drugs and undocumented immigrants across that border—and how it should be done.

IN THE NEWS

The Border Wall

During his run for the U.S. presidency in 2016, Donald Trump promised to build a wall between the southwestern states and Mexico, along the more than 2,000-mile-long border. At first, he assured the American public that Mexico would pay for its construction, an assertion former Mexican president Peña Nieto declared would not happen.

Analysts, advisors, and environmental experts decried the proposal as fiscally prohibitive, ecologically disastrous, and physically impossible. Trump persisted, and, throughout his first term as president, has made multiple attempts to get legislation passed that will fund the building of a border wall.

Sections of the U.S.-Mexico border already have fencing and solid-form barriers to reduce the rates of illegal border crossings. Concerns about how a continuous border wall would affect commercial traffic arose alongside concerns about the environmental impact of such a proposal; multiple animal herds in the region seasonally cross the national border to obtain food and water, and parts of the proposed path of the wall cut through protected lands. There is also the issue of Indian reservations that straddle the border and how their status under American and Mexican law would be affected by a border wall.

The construction of a border wall between Mexico and the United States poses problems on multiple fronts. To get around the environmental obstacles, the Trump administration waived several environmental laws to allow the wall to be built in protected natural areas of Texas. Further, several interest groups, including the American Civil Liberties Union (ACLU) and human and environmental rights groups, state that border communities, public spaces, and natural regions would be negatively impacted. They assert that there are more effective ways to combat smuggling and illegal immigration across the border and have called on the U.S. Congress to reject funding for the border wall at all costs.

Text-Dependent Questions

1. Why did revolutionaries in the early 1800s declare and fight for independence from Spain?

2. What positive and/or negative impacts did Porfirio Díaz's rule have on Mexico's economy and society?

3. What social and economic problems were faced by Mexicans during the 1960s through the 1990s?

Research Project

Research the reforms of Benito Juárez and more recent presidents Felipe Calderon and Enrique Peña Nieto. Write a four- to five-paragraph essay comparing and contrasting their reform initiatives, and provide an analysis of how each man's reforms affected Mexican society.

Mexico in the News in the 21st Century

Mexico Arrests Alleged Zetas Cartel Boss
Al Jazeera, February 9, 2018

Mexico's Congress Votes to Remove Politicians' Legal Immunity
The Guardian, April 20, 2018

Mexican President-Elect Pressures Drugmakers to Contain Prices
Reuters, October 6, 2018

How Mexico and Canada Saved NAFTA
Washington Post, October 8, 2018

Migrating North, but to Mexico, Not the U.S.
New York Times, February 13, 2017

Powerful Earthquake Kills at Least 61 in Mexico
CBC News, September 8, 2017

Mexico's Defense Chief: "We Have Committed Errors" in the War on Drugs
Business Insider, March 31, 2016

These 5 Facts Explain Mexico's Precarious Politics
Time, June 10, 2016

Mexico: Where a Story Becomes Deadly
Al Jazeera, May 28, 2015

Mexico: As Dangerous—and Safe—as Ever
CNN, June 9, 2013

Security Issues

M exico's recent history has seen its course through the twentieth century marked by political and social upheaval, especially through the 1960s and 1970s. Hopes for national security and stability have been hindered by a number of factors, namely expanding and violent drug wars, instances of crime, and high levels of corruption among politicians and business leaders.

Conflicts

Multiple conflicts have plagued Mexico for decades, a legacy of a country defined by revolution, uprisings, and the inability of its government to enact long-term national security policies.

Mexico's war on drugs has turned the nation into the second-deadliest conflict zone, superseded only by Syria, according to the 2017 iteration of the Armed Conflict Survey put out by the International Institute for Strategic

Words to Understand

Graft: The questionable or dishonest acquisition of money or some other personal gain.

Hezbollah: An Islamic political party and paramilitary organization based out of Lebanon.

Impunity: Exemption from punishment or the negative consequences of one's actions.

Interpol: An international network of police forces from 190 world nations, tasked with assisting police in different countries to solve transnational crimes.

Secretariat: A permanent administrative office or department, usually in government, and the staff of that office or department.

Students stand in a burned-out bus during the protests in 1968.

Mexico's Security Issues at a Glance

Military Size	417,550 total personnel
Military Service	18 years for compulsory service, conscript service obligation of 12 months; voluntary enlistment at 16 years with parental consent
Military Spending	$5.5326 billion USD (2017)
Military Branches	Secretariat of National Defense: Army, Mexican Air Force—Secretariat of the Navy: Mexican Navy; includes Naval Air Force, Mexican Naval Infantry Corps (2013)
Illicit Drugs	9.9 percent of population ages 12–65 (2016 estimate)
Active Terrorist Groups (international)	Islamic State in Iraq and Syria (ISIS) and Hezbollah (evidence of financial and ideological support)

Studies. Fatalities from drug-war-related violence reached 23,000 in 2016, a surprising number given that the conflict lacks the use of artillery, tanks, or combat fighters. The violence has also resulted in internal displacement of people within territories under siege by rival drug gangs, and foreign visitors have also been caught in the crossfire.

Disputes with Guatemala stem from issues with their shared border dating all the way back to 1823, when Mexico's southernmost provinces broke away to form the Central American nations of Guatemala, Belize, Honduras, and El Salvador. The border between Mexico and Guatemala is often described as being porous, meaning that low population density creates areas where there is little to no human development between border crossings. This results in avenues where drug traffickers, illegal arms dealers, and illegal immigrants from Central American countries can easily cross into Mexico, putting stress on Mexico's ability to maintain border security and public peace in border states.

The Border with the United States

Between 2016 and 2018, tension between the United States and Mexico rose as American policy makers sought to stem the flow of undocumented immigrants across the U.S.–Mexico border. Earlier policies from U.S. lawmakers and the White House—such as the Immigration Control and Reform Act passed under President Ronald Reagan's administration in 1986, the 2001

The entranceway at the Guatemala–Mexico border at the Hidalgo border crossing.

Since President Donald Trump took office, multiple marches have formed around the country, some in support of building a wall along the border, and others that protest his stance on immigration and DACA and his views on the U.S.–Mexico border.

Development, Relief, and Education for Alien Minors (DREAM) Act, and the Deferred Action for Childhood Arrivals (DACA) program enacted by President Barack Obama's administration in 2012—appeared to promote leniency toward undocumented immigrants and those seeking asylum from violence in Central America.

The crisis along the U.S. border remains in flux. Executive orders from U.S. President Donald Trump and directives from the U.S. Department of Justice attempted to restrict the flow of undocumented immigrants across the border. These embattled policies have resulted in the detention of families, unaccompanied minors, and asylum seekers alike, including the separation of children from their parents at the border. After a public outcry, the White House issued a new executive order to reunite families, but many parents and children remained separated after the order went into effect. Deportations continue at the end of 2018, and no solution to this aspect of the border crisis appears in sight. Further, U.S. President Trump has long promised the construction of a more secure wall along the border, though he remains in a deadlock with the U.S. Congress over obtaining funding for this wall.

Mexico's role in the border crisis, too, has shifted. When a migrant caravan carrying asylum seekers to Southern California was denied entry into the United States in April 2018, Mexico began offering refugee status to some members of the caravan, provided they qualified for this status.

After harrowing images of children in detention centers without their parents were released, the national public was in an uproar. More protests broke out across the country, which forced President Trump to sign an executive order to reunite the families. However, thousands are still separated.

The position of the Mexican Interior Ministry is that such caravans are examples of public demonstration meant to bring attention to the plight of participants; caravan participants are encouraged to disperse and return to their countries of origin, especially if they have not obtained transit visas. The number of asylum cases granted by the Mexican government remains low, according to the Human Rights First organization and Amnesty International.

Refugees vs. Asylum Seekers

Much media coverage has been granted to the topic of asylum seekers and refugees in the wake of the caravans from Central America that have made their way through Mexico to the southern U.S. border in April and October of 2018. But along with this coverage comes confusion over the difference between refugees and asylum seekers and how international law impacts their fates.

Amnesty International defines a refugee as someone who has fled their home country due to fear of persecution because of race, religion, or political affiliation. An asylum seeker, on the other hand, is someone who wishes to obtain international protection from the persecution they have been subjected to in their country of origin. Not all refugees become asylum seekers, but all asylum seekers begin as refugees.

The legal standing of both refugees and asylum seekers is difficult to parse. International law regarding asylum came about after World War II, because the global community had no legal structures in place to handle the waves of migrants fleeing the horrors of warfare and the Holocaust. The UN's passage of the Universal Declaration of Human Rights in 1948 guaranteed the right of any individual to seek asylum, with various world nations adopting and implementing laws accordingly. In the United States, a refugee may apply for asylum whether or not they come into the country through a legal port of entry.

The ongoing vitriol between the presidents of the two nations has also created increased tension over the status of the border wall, among other administrative policies and agreements that could potentially impact Mexico's economic growth in the coming years.

Alliances

Though officially a neutral country when it comes to worldwide conflict. Mexico counts many world nations as allies. By 2010, Mexico held 80 embassies, 69 consulates, and six permanent missions worldwide. It is a founding member of the United Nations and participates in the General Assembly. Mexico is also a member of the North Atlantic Treaty Organization (NATO).

Multiple bilateral and multilateral alliances exist between Mexico and nations from all the world's inhabited continents. Some of its major alliances include the Organization of American States, the Community of Latin American and Caribbean States, **Interpol**, and the Group of Like-Minded Megadiverse Countries.

Regional Relations

Security issues and inequitable distribution of resources have created tension between the Mexican government and many of Mexico's more isolated, rural regions. Mexican states along the southern border with Guatemala and Belize experience high levels of drug trafficking as well as the violence that often accompanies it. Native populations in isolated areas often lack infrastructure, education, and job opportunities. Poverty rates have grown in certain areas, and the government has done little to implement policies to improve living conditions among the nation's poorest people.

Corruption is another issue that creates inequities and threatens perceived stability in many parts of Mexico. The practice of **graft** among

The Embassy of the Sahrawi Arab Democratic Republic (SADR) is located in Mexico City. It is just one of 80 found in Mexico.

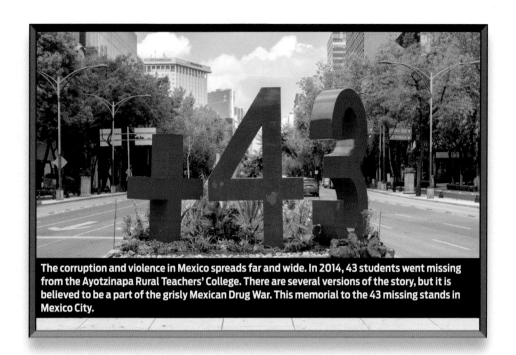

The corruption and violence in Mexico spreads far and wide. In 2014, 43 students went missing from the Ayotzinapa Rural Teachers' College. There are several versions of the story, but it is believed to be a part of the grisly Mexican Drug War. This memorial to the 43 missing stands in Mexico City.

government and municipal officials is widespread, despite an anti-corruption system set up in 2015 to combat the problem. The system is not effective and, at the present time, not well enforced. Grassroots organizations have cropped up to propose solutions to the lack of transparency from many politicians.

The administration of justice and people's trust in the judicial system is also marred by instances of corruption. Some local judiciaries have been infiltrated by drug cartels, allowing cartel bosses and drug traffickers to operate with **impunity**. The police, too, are often involved in aiding and abetting the activities of drug cartels. Public services companies, land and tax administration officials, and customs officials accept corruption as part of the business culture, to the detriment of the people who are served by these groups.

Mexico has identified approximately 345,000 internally displaced persons who have fled government and military responses to the Zapatista uprising in 1994—when an army of 3,000 Mayan guerilla fighters in the southernmost state of Chiapas rebelled against the Mexican government in protest of economic policies they believed would negatively impact the indigenous peoples of Mexico, resulting in a political movement to end the disenfranchisement of Mexico's native population—and drug cartel violence since 2007. Some displaced persons have fled their homes due to violence within and among indigenous groups.

International Relations

Mexico has had to deal with multiple issues with its neighboring nations, including the United States and Guatemala, with whom it shares its northern and southern borders, respectively. Impoverished immigrants from Guatemala and other Central American nations find their way across Mexico's border in search of work. Refugees from El Salvador, Honduras, and Venezuela come into Mexico fleeing economic and political crises and gang violence.

Despite the strain it experiences from the influx of migrants and refugees from its southern neighbors, Mexico has maintained a policy

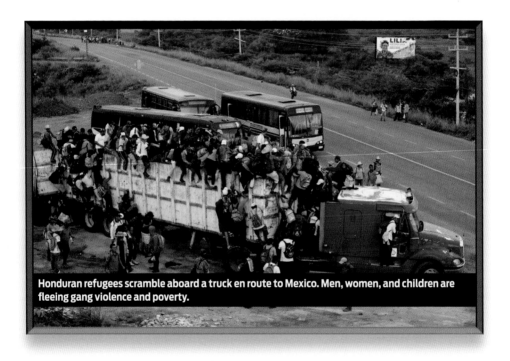
Honduran refugees scramble aboard a truck en route to Mexico. Men, women, and children are fleeing gang violence and poverty.

Violence in Central America and Mexico.

of openness and engagement with nations in Latin America and around the world for the past 20 years. The relationship between Mexico and the United States began to shift, however, after the 2016 U.S. presidential election ended with the ascension of Donald Trump to the White House. Under this administration, U.S. policy toward Mexico targeted immigration and asylum practices in regard to people crossing the border without documentation or visas, as well as economic policies and agreements like NAFTA.

Questions have arisen over how foreign policy may shift under president Andrés Manuel López Obrador. Obrador campaigned on a promise to focus on Mexico's internal affairs—presumably, according to analysts, at the expense of those relationships with the international community.

Human Trafficking

Human rights groups have identified Mexico as a country where human trafficking is on the rise and primarily targets women and children, especially girls between the ages of 10 and 17. Over 3,000 women were reported missing from five of Mexico's 17 states in 2017.

The National Citizen Observatory on Femicide (OCNF) tracks instances of human trafficking, especially that which targets women, and determines that most girls are not abducted at random but are chosen after a period of research. The state of Puebla has one of the highest rates of abductions, and Acapulco is one of the most dangerous cities for women in all of Mexico. Abductions often result in girls and young women being sold into prostitution and, in many cases, the killing of abducted girls.

Reports of abduction, and the murders that often accompany them, rarely end with prosecution, according to OCNF. Authorities may dismiss reports of abduction as girls eloping with boyfriends, and even if a suspect is caught and held, charges may be dropped. Dead ends are common in investigations. All of this reflects a general disregard for the safety of women in Mexico, despite laws that are meant to prevent and prosecute violence against women.

Human trafficking in Mexico also encompasses smugglers who are paid to ferry illegal immigrants seeking asylum across the U.S. border. Those being smuggled include unaccompanied minors, who are sent by family members from Mexico and other Central American countries to protect them from threats of violence and death from gangs and cartels.

Illicit Drugs

Illicit drug trafficking poses a major security threat to Mexico, as several major drug cartels operate within the country and often engage in violent turf wars over control of trafficking routes and production. Mexico is a major drug-producing nation and a major thoroughfare for drug transit from other Central and South American countries. Money laundering as part of the drug trade also occurs at high levels.

Bricks of cocaine are commonly transported across the Mexican border.

The Seemingly Endless Drug War

Mexico has been fighting a war in earnest since 2006, but not against a rival nation. Instead, the government has been engaged in a long-term—and sometimes seemingly endless—war on drug trafficking and the violent drug cartels that profit from the production, transit, and sale of illicit drugs.

Eight major drug cartels operate in Mexico, each with different methods of maintaining control of their territory and share of the market. Some of these groups use extremely violent methods and focus less on drugs than on theft, extortion, and human trafficking; the Los Zetas Cartel, for example, is known for committing massacres of civilians, leaving body parts in public places, and posting about revenge killings on the Internet.

In 2006, president Felipe Calderon began to deploy military personnel and federal police to states where drug-related violence was at a high in an attempt to crack down on drug trafficking. Since then, multiple cartel leaders have been captured or killed, but the cartels fought back with killings of government offi- cials and civilians alike. The war on drugs continued under the administration of president Enrique Peña Nieto, and cross-border raids by Mexican and U.S. law enforcement resulted in the arrests of cartel members. The U.S. Department of Justice has also extradited former cartel leaders from Mexico to face charges of drug trafficking in the United States.

Mexico is the third-largest producer of opium in the world; in addition to raw opium, refined drug products are produced and trafficked as well. Estimates place the annual movement of cocaine to the United States at about 95 percent. Mexico is also a major producer of the drug ecstasy and supplier of heroin and is the largest foreign supplier of the U.S. market for marijuana and methamphetamine.

However, government reports show that Mexico's domestic market for illicit drugs began to increase through the late 2000s. The 2016–2017 National Survey on Drugs, Alcohol, and Tobacco Consumption found that Mexico's highest drug-use rates occur in the states of Baja California, Quintana Roo, Jalisco, Aguascalientes, and Coahuila.

Solutions to Mexico's drug-trafficking problem have been hard to implement. The government runs a huge illicit-crop-eradication program, the largest independent operation in the world. New drug laws signed and enacted in 2009, which made the possession of even small amounts of marijuana, LSD, cocaine, methamphetamine, or heroin no longer a criminal offense, were intended to allow the focus of the war on drugs to shift to dealers and producers rather than users. People convicted of drug possession, instead of being incarcerated, are encouraged (and, after three convictions, required) to enter treatment programs. This shift in policy makes drug use a health issue rather than a criminal one.

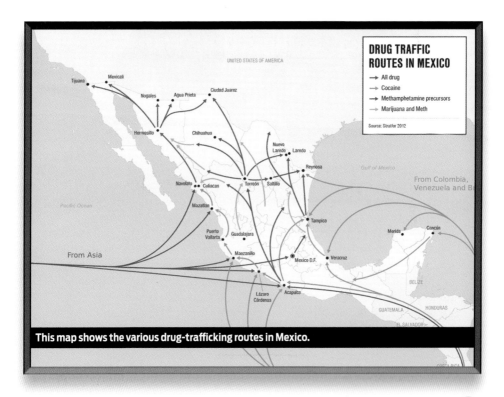

This map shows the various drug-trafficking routes in Mexico.

Military

Mexico's armed forces number approximately 385,000 personnel (274,500 active duty and 110,500 reservists) and include the Mexican army, navy, and air forces. Various **secretariat** departments break down the branches of the military into those dedicated to National Defense, the Army, Mexican Air Force, Navy, Naval Air Force, and Naval Infantry Corps.

The military is a mix of volunteers and conscripts; conscription applies only to the army, whereas service in the navy and air force is voluntary. Mexicans can be conscripted at age 18 but may enlist voluntarily with parental consent at age 16. Only men are eligible for conscription; service for women is voluntary. Any cadets enrolled in a military school from the age of 15 are considered members of the armed forces.

Mexican armed forces during operations in the northeastern part of the country.

The Mexican armed forces are key in the security and stability of the nation, rather than simply being deployed or activated for service in foreign theaters. The government utilizes the military as a counterpart to federal and municipal police in maintaining public peace and collaborating with public-works initiatives. Historically, the military operated at the will of its generals and dealt with rebellions. But the security needs at Mexico's borders, along with the challenges of the violence caused by drug cartels, have changed the mission of the armed forces.

Under government directives, the Mexican armed forces provide security in the south along the border with Guatemala, where the thick rain forest in that region provides cover for drug and arms traffickers. Security along the northern border and in the Gulf of Mexico is largely left to the influence of the U.S. military and border security operations.

Terrorist Groups

Mexico cooperates with the United States in counterterrorism measures due to the large shared border between the two nations and the potential for terrorists to attempt border crossings from Mexico into the United States.

At this time, there are no known international terrorist organizations with active cells in Mexico, though the government identified an increase in terrorist-group sympathizers on social media in December of 2016. Ideological support for ISIS and **Hezbollah** has been identified, and there is some evidence of financial support for Hezbollah occurring in Mexico. Mexico also monitors routes of travel from countries where extremist activity and sympathizers tend to originate, particularly from the Middle East and North Africa.

Several guerilla movements in the 1960s through the 1990s, including Partido de los Pobres, People's Guerilla Group, and Liga Comunista 23 de Septiembre, were responsible for incidents of domestic terrorism. However, these groups disbanded through government actions and the use of extrajudicial executions or forced disappearances. Presently, no domestic terrorist organizations have been identified as operational by the Mexican government, though the several drug cartels in operation throughout the country pose similar threats to national security as domestic terrorism groups would pose.

Some of the counterterrorism steps taken by Mexico include an increase in border-security capabilities, monitoring at airports and migration stations, and the development of an accusatorial justice system designed to investigate and prosecute terrorism and related crimes. Mexico also works to counter financing for terrorism as a member of the Financial Action Task Force (FATF) and the Financial Action Task Force of Latin America. Legislation has also been enacted to deal with terrorist financing, including asset freezing when suspicious activity is identified.

Mexico also works to detect and prosecute extremist propaganda found on the Internet and participates in the Organization of American States Inter-American Committee against Terrorism.

A federal policeman on patrol in the violence-ridden border city of Ciudad Juárez, Mexico.

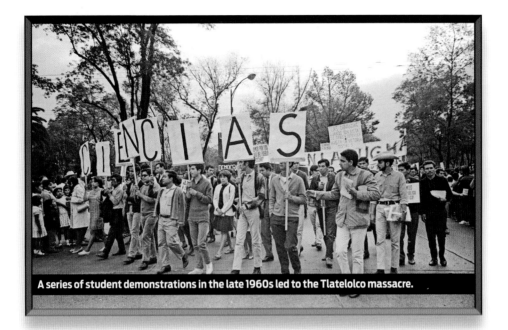

A series of student demonstrations in the late 1960s led to the Tlatelolco massacre.

Text-Dependent Questions

1. What are the recent effects of the U.S.–Mexico border crisis?

2. How have the activities of drug cartels impacted Mexico?

3. How has corruption impacted the security of Mexico and its citizens?

Research Project

Research Mexico's response to the influx of migrants and asylum seekers from Central America, as well as its response to migrants and asylum seekers being turned away at the U.S. border. Write a five- to six-paragraph advisory report addressed to the Mexican president and National Congress analyzing your findings and proposing three possible solutions to the problem.

CHAPTER 2

Government and Politics

Mexico is a federal presidential republic that uses a three-branch system of government made up of an executive, legislative, and judicial branch. The central government oversees national affairs, whereas the administration of regional government occurs within 31 individual states and the Federal District of Mexico City. State governments also follow the model of three independent branches of government.

Constitution

Mexico has seen many iterations of its Constitution since gaining independence from Spain in the early 1800s. The current Constitution was approved on February 5, 1917, following the Mexican Revolution. It guarantees the personal freedoms and civil liberties of Mexican citizens, including protections against discrimination, equality for men and women under the

Words to Understand

Encomienda system: The rigid social hierarchy of Spanish colonies in the Americas, with Spanish-born colonial leaders at the top, followed by Mexican-born residents of Spanish descent, mixed-race people of indigenous and European descent, free peoples of African or African-Amerindian descent, and African slaves.

Peninsulares: Spanish-born members of colonial Mexican society, who held government positions and owned land in New Spain.

Populism: An approach to politics, often with authoritarian elements, that emphasizes the role of ordinary people in a society's government over that of an elite class.

Proportional representation: An electoral system in which political parties gain seats in proportion to the number of votes cast for those seats.

The National Palace is the seat of the federal executive in Mexico.

Mexico's Government and Legal System at a Glance

Independence	September 16, 1810 (declared from Spain, not recognized until 1821)
National Holiday	Independence Day, September 16
National Symbol(s)	Golden eagle; national colors of green, white, and red; Mexican coat of arms (eagle holding a snake in its beak, perched on a cactus)
Constitution	Ratified February 5, 1917
Legal System	Civil law system influenced by U.S. constitutional law; judicial review of legislative acts
Voting Eligibility	18 years of age, universal and compulsory

On February 5, 1917, the new Constitution was approved. This picture shows the Constituent Congress of 1917 pledging allegiance to the newly created Constitution.

law, and freedom of thought and expression. It also establishes Mexico's economic and political principles, including the separation of church and state, specifically in matters of education. The Constitution divides governmental powers among the executive, legislative, and judicial branches at the federal level and defines the terms of service and responsibilities of each.

Amendments to the Constitution are proposed by the National Congress. At least two-thirds of the members of Congress who are present at the time of voting must approve an amendment for it to pass. Further, a majority of the Mexican state legislatures must also vote to approve proposed amendments to the Constitution. The Constitution was last amended in 2017 to establish new procedures to process labor disputes before federal or state labor courts.

Independence

On September 16, 1810, Mexico declared itself independent from Spain, which had held Mexico as part of its vast colonial holdings in the Americas for centuries. Napoleon's conquest of Spain in the early 1800s prompted revolts across Spanish colonies.

In Mexico, the movement for independence initially began with the mestizo population, led by a Catholic priest named Father Hidalgo y Costilla. Hidalgo issued a revolutionary tract that called for the end of

The Bell of Dolores was relocated after Hidalgo's death. Every year, on Independence Day, the president rings the bell in remembrance of Hidalgo.

Spanish rule in Mexico, racial equality, and the redistribution of land holdings. Emboldened by Hidalgo's *grito de Dolores*, or "Cry of Dolores," an army of mestizos rose up against the royalist **peninsulares** who held all governmental control of the colony. This army proved no match for the better-trained and better-equipped Spanish military, and after Hidalgo's capture and death, the revolution for independence seemed to falter. Other peasant leaders took his place, leading armies of native and mixed-race revolutionaries.

The cause for an independent Mexico was then taken up by the Creoles, people of Spanish descent who were born in Mexico. Despite often being wealthy and having a high level of social status, Creoles could not hold political office or other governmental jobs due to the rigidity of the **encomienda system**. When more liberal leaders took power in Spain in 1820, the new government promised to reform both governmental and societal practices in Mexico. Many Creoles believed this would be their chance to improve their political position but still maintain their privileged position in Mexican society.

The war lasted until 1821. Revolutionary leader Vicente Guerrero negotiated with Royalist leader Agustin de Iturbide for a plan to establish Mexico's independence. The plan called for Mexico to become an independent constitutional monarchy with a member of the Bourbon family at the helm. Mexicans of Spanish descent would be considered social equals to Spanish-born residents, whereas Mexicans of mixed or pure Amerindian bloodlines would still have lesser rights.

Iturbide still had to defeat Royalist forces, which opposed Mexican independence. The Spanish viceroy lacked the money, troops, and provisions to hold off or defeat Iturbide's army and surrendered in the summer of 1821. Spain finally recognized Mexico's independence on September 27.

Legal System

The legal system in Mexico exists as a civil law system, highly influenced by the precedence of U.S. constitutional law. Legislative acts come under judicial review before they can be implemented.

Mexico also accepts the jurisdiction of the International Criminal Court (ICC), which prosecutes international criminal cases. It also accepts compulsory jurisdiction of the International Court of Justice (ICJ), which settles arguments between nations, but does so with reservations.

Political Parties

Mexico has nine major political parties that currently operate within the country, representing a wide range of political and social perspectives:

- Institutional Revolutionary Party (Partido Revolucionario Institucional—PRI)
- Labor Party (Partido del Trabajo—PT)

- Mexican Green Ecological Party (Partido Verde Ecologista de Mexico—PVEM)

- Movement for National Regeneration (Movimiento Regeneracion Nacional—MORENA)

- National Action Party (Partido Accion Nacional—PAN)

- New Alliance Party (Partido Nueva Alianza—PNA/PANAL)

- Party of the Democratic Revolution (Partido de la Revolucion Democratica—PRD)

- Social Encounter Party (Partido Encuentro Social—PES)

- Citizens Movement (Movimiento Cuidadano—MC)

For years, the Institutional Revolutionary Party (PRI) and the National Action Party (PAN) produced popular candidates for government office.

The National Revolutionary Party was founded by Plutarco Elias Calles (pictured). He was the president of Mexico from 1924 to 1928.

The PRI, for instance, won every presidential election between its establishment in 1929 until the 1982 election. PAN emerged in 1939 as the opposition party. The majority of governorships, positions in state legislatures, and local government officials still come from PRI.

Growing issues with food shortages, rising crime rates, and economic fluctuations over the past two decades have made more Mexicans doubtful of the political abilities of candidates from these traditionally powerful parties. As the second decade of the twenty-first century draws to a close, the voice and influence of parties that may once have been on the extreme left of Mexico's political spectrum have begun to take center stage.

In the 2018 election cycle, the Movement for National Regeneration (MORENA) held the strongest showing. MORENA's candidate for president, Andrés Manuel López Obrador, won with 53.2 percent of the overall vote. In the legislature, MORENA claimed 58 out of 128 seats in the Senate and 193 out of 500 seats in the Chamber of Deputies.

Andrés Manuel López Obrador on the campaign trail.

The Rise of Populism in Mexico

Worldwide, a rise in **populism** is changing the face of politics and, with it, elections and governments. Populist movements usually include the mobilization of groups that have been marginalized or excluded, whereas opponents face potential obstacles to political agency. Populist governments often include criticism of—and, in extreme cases, the revocation of—political systems that restrain the powers of the executive.

Historically, populism's most successful candidates, politicians, parties, and interest groups came from the right of the political spectrum. But the growth of populism in Mexico has come from the left instead.

Populism in Latin America is not new—leaders like Venezuela's Hugo Chávez gained and wielded great power throughout the 2000s. The movement reemerged in various parts of the region in the early to mid-2010s. In Mexico, the growing popularity of populism facilitated the rise of Andrés Manuel López Obrador, popularly referred to by his initials, AMLO.

Certain social and economic conditions made the political field ripe for Obrador's rise to prominence. Many Mexican voters, especially those among the working class, have long felt disenfranchised at worst, or that their votes simply do not matter at best. Corruption can be found throughout government institutions, and violence and crime rates are increasing. With nearly half the population living in poverty, there is little opportunity for upward social mobility. The political climate and the timing were right for Obrador, whose message resonated with Mexicans frustrated by the perceived inability of previous leaders to strengthen Mexico's economy, end corruption, and address the causes of violence that plague the country.

The Executive Branch

The executive branch of Mexico's government consists of the chief of state, head of government, and the cabinet. The president acts as both chief of state and head of government and is directly elected by a simple majority popular vote for a single term of six years. In addition to the duties of chief of state and head of government, the president also acts as the commander in chief of the armed forces. The most recent presidential election was held on July 1, 2018, and resulted in the election of Andrés Manuel López Obrador. December 1, 2018, marked the beginning of Obrador's term in office.

A presidential cabinet meeting takes place under former president Enrique Peña Nieto.

Andrés Manuel López Obrador wins the 2018 election.

The president appoints members of the cabinet, though the appointments of some cabinet positions require consent from the Senate. These include the appointment of the attorney general, the head of the Bank of Mexico, and senior treasury officials. The president also appoints, with approval, Supreme Court justices, various diplomats, and high-ranking military officers, as well as the mayor of the Federal District (Mexico City). The president can also issue executive decrees, called *reglamentos*, that are similar to executive orders in the United States in that they hold the effect of law once implemented.

There is no position of vice president, so the legislature must designate a provisional successor should the president die in office or become incapacitated. Historically, the executive branch dominates the government—up to 90 percent of proposed bills that come before the legislature originate with the president—though this imbalance of power has lessened since the end of the twentieth century. For much of the 1900s, presidents heavily influenced or directly decided on the outcomes of state and local affairs.

The Legislative Branch

The National Congress (Congreso de la Union) operates as a bicameral legislature made up of the Senate and the Chamber of Deputies. Both chambers discuss and approve legislation and the ratification of high-level presidential appointments. Congress has the power to pass laws, impose taxes, declare war, approve the national budget, approve or reject treaties with foreign nations, and ratify diplomatic appointments.

Powers shared between the two chambers include the establishment of committees to discuss government issues, question officials, and study and recommend bills; joint committees may be formed to develop compromise versions of bills, if a disagreement arises between the chambers. In cases of impeachment, the two chambers convene in a General Congress.

The upper chamber, the Senate (Camara de Senadores), consists of 128 total members; 96 senators are directly elected by simple majority vote

Meeting places for Congress include the Senate Building in Mexico City.

in multi-seat constituencies, and the remaining 32 senators are directly elected in a nationwide constituency by a proportional representation vote. Members of the Senate serve six-year terms in office. The Senate deals with matters of foreign affairs, including international agreements, and confirms presidential appointments.

The lower chamber, the Chamber of Deputies (Camara de Diputados), has 500 total seats. Three hundred members are directly elected by a simple majority vote for single-seat constituencies. The remaining 200 seats are directly elected in a nationwide constituency by a proportional representation vote. Members of the Chamber of Deputies serve three-year terms. The Chamber addresses matters related to the national budget and public expenditures and has the power to prosecute in cases of impeachment (the Senate acts as the jury in impeachment cases).

During the 2018 election cycle, both the Senate and the Chamber of Deputies had their seats up for a vote. Incumbent senators were eligible for a second term, and deputies became eligible to serve up to four consecutive terms. Prior to this, members of the legislature could not be immediately reelected for the succeeding term.

The Judicial Branch

Mexico's judicial branch is made up of the Supreme Court of Justice (Suprema Corte de Justicia de la Nacion), which operates as the highest court in the nation, the Electoral Tribunal of the Federal Judiciary, and several subordinate courts.

The Supreme Court of Justice consists of the chief justice and 11 justices and is organized into panels that deal with civil, criminal, administrative, or labor issues. Justices are nominated by the president and approved by two-thirds of the members present in the Senate. Supreme Court justices serve for life.

The Electoral Tribunal of the Federal Judiciary is organized into a superior court with seven judges, including a court president. Its sworn task is to oversee elections. Five regional courts, each with three judges, are also part of the Electoral Tribunal. Superior and regional court judges are nominated by the Supreme Court of Justice and elected by a two-thirds majority vote in the Senate. Superior court judges elect the court president from among its members for a four-year term of office. Other superior and regional court judges serve nine-year terms, with elections being staggered.

Subordinate courts are divided between courts at the federal level and state- and district-level courts. Federal subordinate courts include circuit courts, collegiate courts, and unitary courts. Most cases of a serious nature are brought before federal judges and typically do not include the assistance of juries.

Inside one of the chambers of the Mexican Supreme Court.

Text-Dependent Questions

1. What are some of the freedoms and civil liberties guaranteed by the Mexican Constitution?

2. What has caused many Mexican voters to turn away from traditional political parties since the early 2000s?

3. What are the features of populist movements? What has been the focus of populist leader Andrés Manuel López Obrador?

Research Project

Research the political views and policies of Mexico's presidents and ruling parties from 1930 to 2018. Write a five- to six-paragraph essay explaining the policies seen through the twentieth century into the twenty-first century and examining the effectiveness of the implementation of these policies. Extension: Evaluate the social, economic, and political factors that influenced changes in governmental policy, and create a visual (e.g., a time line or infographic) illustrating your findings.

Economy

Mexico's economy is the 11th largest in the world, with a gross domestic product (GDP) in 2017 standing at approximately $2.428 trillion. Since the advent of the North American Free Trade Agreement (NAFTA) in 1994, government policies have turned the economy's orientation toward manufacturing rather than focusing on agriculture. Overall economic growth began to slow in 2013, despite reforms by President Peña Nieto that were intended to bolster the economy. Falling oil production and weak oil prices, issues with low productivity and a large sector that informally employs over half of Mexico's workforce, and corruption have all impacted economic growth. (Informal employment results in a loss of government revenue in the form of taxes, underfunded social services, and lack of workers' access to labor protections.) The real growth rate of the GDP dropped over a full percentage point between 2015 and 2017, from 3.3 percent growth to 2 percent growth.

Mexico and the United States have long held close economic ties, and the United States is Mexico's top trading partner and shares supply chains. The uncertain future of NAFTA under the shifting policies of U.S. President Donald Trump helped create vulnerability in Mexico's economy following the 2016 U.S. election. The inauguration of Mexico's new president, Andrés Manuel López Obrador, in December 2018 also brings the future of the

Words to Understand

Free-floating currency: A currency whose value is determined by the free market, changing according to supply and demand for that currency.

Money market trading: The trading of financial instruments with high liquidity and short-term maturities, intended for short-term borrowing and lending.

Tariff: A tax or fee placed on imported or exported products.

Mexico City is the financial center of Mexico.

Mexico's Economy at a Glance

Currency	Mexican peso (MXN); 2018 exchange rate: 18.68 pesos per U.S. dollar
Inflation Rate	4.9 percent (August 2018)
Labor Force	54.51 million; 13.4 percent in agriculture, 24.1 percent in industry, 61.9 percent in services
Overall Unemployment	3.5 percent (October 2018)
Youth Unemployment (ages 15–24)	6.8 percent (2017 estimate)
Imports	Metalworking machines, steel mill products, agricultural machinery, electrical equipment, auto parts for assembly/repair, aircraft and aircraft parts, plastics, natural gas and oil products
Import Partners	United States 46.4 percent, China 17.7 percent, Japan 4.3 percent (2017)
Export	Manufactured goods, electronics, vehicles and auto parts, oil and oil products, silver, plastics, fruits, vegetables, coffee, cotton
Export Partners	United States 79.9 percent (2017)
Industries	Food and beverages, tobacco, chemicals, iron and steel, petroleum, mining, textiles, clothing, motor vehicles, consumer durables, tourism

The Mexican president, U.S. president, and Canadian prime minister signed a draft of the North American Free Trade Agreement in October 1992.

U.S.–Mexican trade agreements into question, because Obrador has vowed to prioritize domestic production over the export of Mexican-made goods.

Currency and Banking System

Mexico uses the Mexican peso (MXN or MX$) as its currency. One peso equals 100 centavos, or Mexican cents. Bank notes come in denominations of 20, 50, 100, 200, 500, and 1,000 pesos. Peso coins in denominations of one, two, and five Mexican pesos are also in circulation. Mexican cents are minted in denominations of five, 10, 20, and 50 centavos. Considered a **free-floating currency** in foreign-exchange markets, the value of the Mexican peso changes daily. In May 2019, the exchange rate was 19.16 Mexican pesos per one U.S. dollar.

The Bank of Mexico is the country's national bank. Established in 1925, it operates out of Mexico City. The Bank of Mexico is responsible for issuing currency and controlling interest rates, a role that has helped stabilize the value of the Mexican peso. Prior to 2008, a method called the Corto was used to control interest rates by keeping the banking system short of its daily monetary demand. After 2008, the Bank of Mexico changed its methods to mimic the U.S. Federal Reserve Bank.

As of September 2017, 48 commercial banks operated throughout Mexico, offering services like deposit accounts, corporate finance, trusts and mutual funds, consumer and commercial lending, foreign exchange, and **money market trading**. Seven major banks—Bancomer, Stantander,

A wallet filled with pesos.

The Bank of Mexico building in Mexico City.

Banorte, Banamex, HSBC, Inbursa, and Scotia Bank—hold assets that, combined, give them control of almost 80 percent of the market share. Other than Banorte, these major banks have come under the auspices of various foreign banks.

Mexico also has a number of banks that are referred to as development banks, designed to fill financing shortfalls in the commercial banking system. Development banks are government-owned, including Nacional Financiera (Nafinsa) and the National Bank for International Trade (Bancomext). These banks lend through commercial banks and credit unions, and finance various types of businesses and economic sectors in need of support.

Individuals and companies can also use nontraditional banks, either regulated or nonregulated, for the purposes of financial activities such as currency exchange, leasing, and lending.

President Peña Nieto announced a series of financial reforms in early 2014 with the aims of redefining the purpose of development banks, encouraging lower rates on financing, and promoting financing from private sources. By the end of 2017, these reforms were slowly bringing down borrowing costs and increasing overall access to credit.

Labor Force

Mexico's labor force numbered approximately 54.51 million people in 2017. Of the labor force, 13.4 percent work in agriculture, 24.1 percent work in industry, and 61.9 percent work in services. Increased productivity among

A farmer harvests blue agave for tequila production in Jalisco, Mexico.

workers, higher rates of immigration to Mexico, and government support for increased employment has helped the labor force grow over the past decade. The growth in the labor force is also a result of NAFTA, which created an atmosphere in which foreign companies saw the establishment of Mexican production sites as a financial boon, thanks to the ability to import materials and export finished goods without paying **tariffs**.

Labor laws have made it easier for both employers and employees. Federal labor laws allow for employee trial periods and training periods as part of the hiring process, and companies have more flexibility in how wages can be paid out. Anti-harassment laws also reduce on-the-job stress for employees, because they help create more positive work cultures where bullying and sexual harassment will not be tolerated.

Immigrants come to Mexico from Asia, Africa, Europe, and South America. Many American citizens reside in Mexico as well. Federal labor laws and migration laws entice highly educated workers from around the globe to relocate to Mexico, especially scientists, artists, professors, and executives who arrive with prearranged employment. Foreign workers can expect the same treatment under the law as Mexican nationals. Further, all immigrants can access Mexico's health-care and educational systems.

Poverty

After several years of declining poverty rates from 2003 to 2009, the number of Mexicans living below the poverty line experienced a sudden spike in 2012. The Espinosa Yglesias Study Center released a report in

A homeless man sleeps on a bench in Cancún.

May of 2018 stating that approximately 46.3 percent of Mexicans lived in poverty, with about 7.6 million of those people living in extreme poverty. According to this study, the general lack of economic mobility in Mexico means that seven out of 10 people born into poverty will also die in poverty.

Factors that account for the high level of poverty include a lack of quality employment and access to educational opportunities, as well as a lack of health care and social security in certain areas and among certain populations. Regions along the southern Pacific coast typically have the highest poverty rates; for example, Chiapas is the poorest state in the entire country, with a poverty rate of 76.2 percent. The second poorest state is Oaxaca, with a poverty rate of 66.8 percent.

Mexico's National Council for the Evaluation of Social Development Policy (CONEVAL) defines people living in poverty as those who earn below an established "well-being threshold" and who live with one or more social deprivations. In 2014, the well-being threshold for urban areas was set at 2,542 pesos ($157.70) per month, whereas the well-being threshold in rural areas stood at 1,615 pesos. Extreme poverty has been defined as those living on an income at or under 1,243 pesos in urban areas and 868 pesos in rural areas.

Government programs exist to assist those living in poverty, such as a conditional cash-transfer program and the expansion of health-care coverage. But Mexico's stagnant economic growth rate has made it difficult for poverty-reduction efforts to be effective. Though Mexico has increased services to the poor, the incomes of the poor have not increased. Poverty rates will not begin to drop until economic growth and development improve.

People who belong to indigenous populations are more likely to experience poverty than their mestizo countrymen. The majority of people living in extreme poverty come from the indigenous population.

Agriculture

Mexico has long been a producer of foodstuffs, for domestic consumption as well as export. Major agricultural products include produce like corn, wheat, soybeans, rice, various types of beans, coffee, tropical fruits, and tomatoes. Beef, poultry, and dairy products are also produced, alongside wood products (e.g., paper, pulp, plywood, lumber, and other products that come from sawmills) and cotton.

The agricultural sector has recently shifted to a more market-oriented model, and the balance of trade between Mexico and the United States—Mexico's principle agricultural trading partner—favored Mexico by 2016. Bilateral agricultural trade between the two nations saw a fivefold increase after NAFTA went into effect in 1994. A highly charged political climate developed after the 2016 U.S. election and has been further fed by potential policy changes under the incoming Mexican president, as both countries

An elderly man begs for money in Chiapas.

Farmers sow their corn fields with help from their donkey.

seek to bolster domestic production and consumption in agriculture and other industries. In 2003, Mexico imposed restrictions on beef products imported from Canada due to concerns about bovine spongiform encephalopathy, better known as mad cow disease. The ban was finally lifted in 2016.

Mexican farmers face a number of challenges today, including tariffs on exports as well as the impact of climate change on the ability to grow and raise agricultural products. New methods of farming, like silvopastoralism (growing crops alongside trees), crop rotation, and carbon farming, that may circumvent the impact of climate change are being implemented by some Mexican farmers in an attempt to keep production levels stable and effective. Domestic consumption of Mexican agricultural products continues to grow, especially in terms of dairy, poultry, beef, and pork products. The demand for organic food products has also grown in Mexico.

Industries

Mexico's workforce has become highly specialized in recent years, as a shift toward manufacturing has brought production sites to the country for everything from aircraft parts to automobile components to electronics.

One major industry that has seen expansion is metal fabrication, especially steel. As of June 2018, over 70 metal-fabrication sites existed across

Finding solutions to climate change.

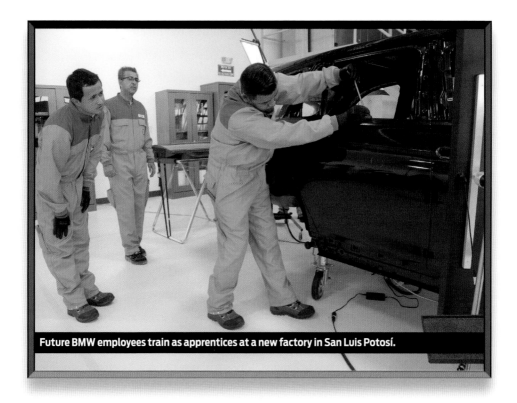

Future BMW employees train as apprentices at a new factory in San Luis Potosí.

Mexico. The automotive parts industry is the fifth largest in the world, and Mexico produces the most vehicle components and automobile models for companies like Audi, Chrysler, and General Motors. The growth of the automotive parts industry is due, in part, to the specialized experience many Mexican workers have gained in the past decade. Manufacturers of electronic devices have also turned to Mexican production sites to increase their supply. Again, specialization and training programs have created highly skilled Mexican workers, and economic experts expect the number of workers in the field of electronics to increase as the millennial generation ages.

Although traditional industries like textile and apparel manufacturing still exist in Mexico, diversification has increased the presence of a number of other major industries. In addition to metal fabrication, electronic devices, and automotive parts, Mexican manufacturing also includes medical devices, appliances, furniture, aerospace products, and clean energy products such as solar panels and wind turbines.

Tourism is also a major industry, and the nation is the top international destination for American vacationers. Tourists from other Latin American countries choose to travel to Mexico as well, and the number of visitors to Mexico is expected to reach up to 40 million by the end of 2018.

IN THE NEWS

Security of Mexico's Tourism Industry under Threat

The tourism industry in Mexico saw record levels of revenue in 2017, and statistics from the first quarter of 2018 proved that revenue was continuing to climb. Tourist hotspots like Acapulco, Cancún, and Playa del Carmen draw visitors from around the world, especially the United States, and an estimated 10 million Mexicans earn their living directly or indirectly from tourism.

But issues with violence and crime that plague Mexico are impacting the tourism industry. Cities like Cancún and Acapulco have seen foreign tourists targeted by gunmen and bombings. Though the industry as a whole remains strong, the rise in instances of violent crime creates security problems for major tourist destinations.

In January 2018, the U.S. State Department issued "do not travel" advisories for five Mexican states along the border between the two countries, though the advisory did not include Mexico's biggest tourism destinations. Both nations have cited rising crime rates as the reason behind the advisories, not necessarily that instances of violent crime are directly affecting tourists.

Still, worries about organized crime that targets foreign visitors may impact future growth of the tourism industry. Communities like Playa del Carmen and Cancún have supported the U.S. advisory, believing the Mexican government will not take security issues seriously unless it sees a potential impact on tourism.

Commodities

Mexico is a producer of several commodity exports, including crude petroleum, gold, tropical fruits, tomatoes, and silver. Commodity imports include refined petroleum, aluminum, soybeans, wheat, and corn.

As the world's fifth-largest exporter of crude petroleum worldwide, Mexico holds a 5.6 percent share of the market, and exports of this commodity primarily end up in American markets. Other important export markets for Mexican crude petroleum include Spain, Japan, and India. Mexico is also the leading exporter of tropical fruits and tomatoes, again with the majority of exports going to the United States.

The markets for gold and silver from Mexico have both seen a decline in the last several years. Mexico remains the leader for silver exports with a 10.5 percent share of the global market. But Mexico holds less than a 5 percent share of the global gold market, and its export numbers have declined almost 40 percent in the past five years.

Imports and Exports

Top exported goods from Mexico include electronics, vehicles and automotive parts, oil and oil products, fruits and vegetables, coffee, cotton, gold and silver, and manufactured goods. Most of Mexico's exports go to the United States, followed by Canada, China, Germany, and Japan.

A petroleum tanker sits in the bay in Acapulco.

A man harvests coffee beans for export.

Major imports come from the United States, China, Japan, Germany, and South Korea and include steel-mill products and metalworking machinery, agricultural machinery, electrical equipment, automotive parts for assembly or repair, aircraft and aircraft parts, plastics, and natural gas and refined oil products.

Mexico has trade agreements with dozens of world nations. These include the North American Free Trade Agreement (NAFTA); the Mexico–EU Free Trade Agreement that establishes free trade with the European Union; the Japan–Mexico Free Trade Agreement; the G3 agreement with Colombia and Venezuela; the Pacific Alliance with Chile and Peru; and the Central America–Mexico Free Trade Agreement with Guatemala, Costa Rica, Honduras, El Salvador, and Nicaragua.

The Trans-Pacific Partnership (TPP) was a free trade agreement originally intended to push back against China's influence in the Pacific. Negotiations experienced a blow when the United States withdrew from the agreement in early 2017. The remaining nations—Australia, Mexico, Brunei, Malaysia, Japan, New Zealand, Peru, Singapore, Chile, Canada,

and Vietnam—have delayed ratification of the deal while alternatives are reviewed and the pros and cons are evaluated.

NAFTA

The United States has long been the leading trade partner with Mexico, and NAFTA, a trade agreement that also includes Canada, has boosted trade between the three largest nations on the North American continent. Around 80 percent of Mexico's imports go to the United States and around 5.4 percent to Canada. A rising populist, nationalistic trend in the political climate of the United States has prompted leaders, including President Donald Trump, to consider withdrawing from NAFTA and implementing tariffs that would raise the price of Mexican goods in American markets.

In early October 2018, the three countries agreed to a revised version of NAFTA that will be called the United States–Mexico–Canada Agreement (USMCA) and will go into effect in 2020, after the leaders of all three countries sign and the legislatures of Canada and Mexico approve the new agreement. One stated goal of the USMCA is to ensure more automotive

In 2018, President Donald Trump, President Enrique Peña Nieto, and Prime Minister Justin Trudeau signed a new agreement called the United States–Mexico–Canada Agreement (USMCA) that will replace NAFTA.

parts are manufactured in North America (up to 75 percent from the previous threshold of 62.5 percent), and that by 2020, at least 30 percent of the work done on vehicles must be completed by workers earning at least $16 an hour. Economists believe these changes will help some North American workers, but the changes may also push up the cost of vehicles and potentially end the production of some small cars that would be too expensive to produce under the new requirements.

Energy

Energy demand in Mexico has grown by 25 percent since 2000, with consumption of electricity growing by almost half. Fuel for energy production comes primarily from oil and natural gas. Over 70 percent of Mexico's electricity comes from fossil fuels and another 2.1 percent from nuclear power plants. But renewable energy sources have begun to gain ground since 2016, due to private-sector willingness to invest in solar and wind capacity. About 8.5 percent of Mexico's electricity comes from renewable sources.

Comprehensive energy reforms enacted since 2013 change the structures that control the energy sector, allowing for investment in both traditional energy sources as well as low-carbon sources. Mexico has committed to a clean energy target, submitting a pledge to reduce the nation's carbon emissions even before negotiations began for the Paris Climate Agreement in 2015. Renewable and clean energy sources include wind turbines, hydropower, geothermal power, solar power, and plant-based energy sources like ethanol, fuel wood, and bagasse, the organic residue from the sugarcane industry.

Surveys from 2012 showed that 99 percent of Mexico's population have access to electricity in their homes. In urban areas, 100 percent of people have access to electricity, whereas the rate in rural areas stands at approximately 97 percent.

Text-Dependent Questions

1. How have Mexico's industries and labor force changed in the past decade?

2. What impact is the USMCA expected to have on Mexico? How does this compare to the impact of NAFTA on Mexico's economy?

3. What factors impact the poverty rate in Mexico? Who is most likely to be affected by these factors, and why?

Research Project

Choose one of Mexico's growing manufacturing industries, and research its development, growth, and future revenue projections. Writing from the perspective of an economic advisor to a fictional company CEO, compose a two- to three-page report outlining the steps the company should take to become a competitive member of that industry, including production costs and investments, training programming for workers, and potential outcomes.

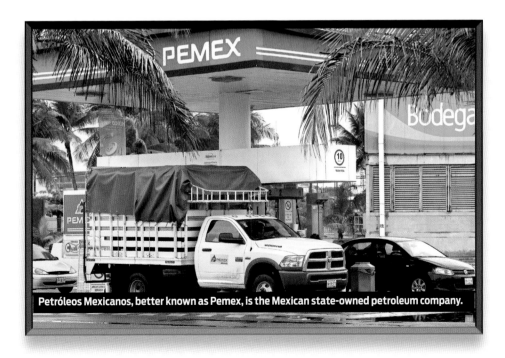

Petróleos Mexicanos, better known as Pemex, is the Mexican state-owned petroleum company.

Quality of Life

Chapter **4**

Despite being the second-largest economy in Latin America, Mexico has historically struggled to create a stable quality of life in which all citizens' needs are met. High unemployment goes hand in hand with high poverty rates, especially among the indigenous population. Corruption has also plagued Mexico's political machinations for decades, and rising crime rates in major urban centers greatly impact people's personal safety and well-being.

Despite these challenges, Mexico has made great strides in the past 10 years to improve the areas of education, health care, and job prospects. Its citizens also hold a positive level of civic engagement and sense of community.

Basic Human Needs

In terms of basic human needs, Mexico's government attempts to provide basic medical care and nutrition to its citizens. Members of the National Congress have worked since 2016 to develop and implement an initiative intended to improve citizens' income, with the aim of also improving

Words to Understand

Dengue fever: A tropical disease transmitted by mosquitoes, causing debilitating symptoms including sudden fever and acute joint pain.

Food insecurity: Being without reliable access to nutritious food at an affordable price and in sufficient quantity.

Vocational: In education, training that prepares people for work in various jobs, such as in a trade or craft or as a technician.

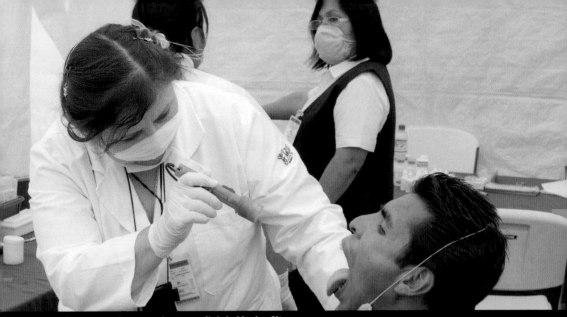

A doctor examines a patient at a clinic in Mexico City.

Mexico's Quality of Life at a Glance

Life Expectancy at Birth	76.1 years (73.3 years for males; 79 years for females)
Maternal Mortality Rate	38 deaths/100,000 live births (2015)
Child Mortality Rate	11.6 deaths/1,000 live births
Mother's Average Age at First Birth	21.3 years of age
Access to Contraception	66.9 percent of population
Obesity	28.9 percent of adult population
Poverty	46.3 percent of total population
Improved Drinking Water Source	96.1 percent of population (97.2 percent urban areas, 92.1 percent rural areas)
Improved Sanitation Facility Access	85.2 percent of population (88 percent urban areas, 74.5 percent rural areas)
Electricity Access	99 percent of the population (100 percent in urban areas, 97 percent in rural areas)
Years of Education	13 years
Mobile Cellular Access	92 subscriptions per 100 inhabitants (2017 estimate)
Internet Access	59.5 percent of population (July 2016 estimate); 14 broadband subscriptions per 100 inhabitants (2017)
Broadcast Media	821 television stations and 1,745 radio stations, mostly privately owned

their ability to access necessities like food. They view the ability to earn an income that provides for an individual's basic survival as both a need and a right. However, issues with equitable and effective implementation have resulted in inconsistent effects on the overall health and well-being of the population.

Nutrition and Basic Medical Care

A 2012 national survey on nutrition determined that almost 18 percent of Mexicans experience moderate **food insecurity** and over 10 percent experience severe food insecurity. Isolated rural populations, made up mostly of indigenous groups, are most likely to suffer from food insecurity due to a lack of access to national programs and a high level of poverty. Estimates from 2015 placed the percentage of children under the age of five who were considered medically underweight at just below 4 percent. This rate stood at almost 11 percent in 1988 and had fallen to just under 3 percent in 2012.

Obesity is a problem for Mexicans as well—obesity levels tripled between 1982 and 2012. Almost 29 percent of adults were considered obese in 2016, and over 34 percent of children between the ages of five and 11 were found to be overweight or obese in 2012. The dietary patterns of Mexican adults provide insight into the prevalence of obesity, specifically

Women from the Huichol tribe await medical exams and food in Jalisco.

high intakes of refined foods, sweets, and animal products. The high rate of consumption of soft drinks has prompted the Mexican government to issue a tax on them in an attempt to reduce consumption.

Mexico's health-care system, like many other aspects of Mexican society, has seen some changes over the past several years. At present, Mexicans are able to choose between public and private health-care plans that are linked to their own doctors, pharmacies, and health-care centers. Private health care is better than public health care, but it is also more expensive. Urban centers like Mexico City, Monterrey, and Guadalajara have the highest-rated hospitals in the country, especially when it comes to serious conditions that may require major procedures like surgery. Both private and public employees are covered by a social health security system that guarantees government-provided coverage, and the Ministry of Health ensures access to adequate medical care for unemployed citizens.

Water and Sanitation

Most Mexicans have access to a safe drinking water source (96.1 percent) and appropriate sanitation facilities (85.2 percent). Urban areas have better infrastructure and are far more likely to have improved water and sanitation sources than rural areas. Access to clean drinking water and

Patients wait in line to see the doctor at a health clinic in Mexico City.

A water delivery truck prepares to make its rounds. As of 2017, nine million people still lacked access to potable water.

proper sanitation and sewage systems is essential to maintain the health of a community.

In 2011, Mexico invested $600 million to improve its water and sanitation infrastructure for rural communities and in its public schools. The investment sought to address the incidences of waterborne diseases that can impact a child's school attendance. The Water, Sanitation, and Hygiene in Basic Education Program targeted areas with high-risk factors for waterborne illnesses alongside high enrollment numbers.

Despite the relatively high number of people who have access to water and sanitation facilities, nine million people lacked access to potable water and 10.2 million had no basic sanitation infrastructure in their homes, according to a 2017 report from the National Water Commission. Water-delivery services have been instrumental in providing water to certain areas, including Mexico City. Measures, such as the National Waters Law, National Waters Program, and the establishment of the National Waters Commission (CONAGUA), have been taken to address the mismanagement of water and to improve the treatment of wastewater in large cities. Some experts state that water and sanitation safety is the responsibility not just of the government but of the members of the communities as well.

Shelter

The Organization for Economic Cooperation and Development (OECD), of which Mexico is a part, estimates that Mexican households spend up to 21 percent of their disposable income on housing. For many families, this is the largest expenditure in their budget, especially when all associated costs—rent, utilities, repairs, and furnishings—are combined. Many families live in houses or apartments containing only one room per person, which is below the 1.8 room average in most OECD countries. This means that many Mexicans live in crowded conditions, which contributes to health and wellness problems as well as issues with water and sanitation systems.

Living conditions are particularly difficult in cities, given the rapid pace of urbanization in recent years. Mexican authorities historically focused on the building of houses rather than urban planning. Recent implementation of the National Urban Development Program seeks to improve the physical and social conditions in Mexican neighborhoods with a more explicit focus on housing and the urban environment.

Even with this shift in policies, many people in Mexico's largest cities live in overcrowded neighborhoods referred to as "shantytowns" or must

Houses in Guanajuato are built extremely close to one another upon a hillside.

An isolated shack in San Luis Potosí.

Life in a slum of Mexico.

cram into so-called micro-apartments when they can afford nothing else. Although some realize this is the best they can hope for and plan for a better future, the immediate effects of living in such close quarters can include failure in school, child abuse, tension, and depression and anxiety. These conditions, compounded by the stress of long commute times to work or school, exacerbate the potential for conflict within families.

Personal Safety

Reports of crime and gang-related activity in Mexico sometimes flood the news cycle, which begs the question of how safe Mexico is for both its residents and visitors. High-profile homicides, the activity of drug cartels, and relatively rare instances of violence against tourists are all of concern in a country that struggles with national security in general, alongside issues of corruption among the nation's security forces and police. Only half of people living in Mexico report feeling safe when walking alone at night.

Homicide rates represent the extremes of crime, but they are a reliable indicator of a country's safety level due to the rate at which they are reported to the police. Mexico's homicide rate is almost 18 per 100,000 inhabitants, the highest among OECD countries and much higher than the OECD average of 3.6 murders per 100,000 inhabitants. Other common crimes include robbery and sexual assault.

Drug-related violence occurs in areas where major drug cartels vie for control of trafficking routes to the United States. Typically, such violence does not target everyday citizens or visitors, but people may inadvertently find themselves caught in the crossfire of these turf wars if they live in or visit areas where drug cartels and narcotics markets are active. Many countries, including the United States, have issued travel advisories for Mexican states where turf wars between drug cartels have flared up in recent years.

Violence against women has proven enough of a problem that Mexico implemented the Integrated Program to Prevent, Address, Sanction, and Eradicate Violence, beginning in 2014. The program looks at the way national policies and strategies are designed and coordinates action across all levels of government to combat instances of violence against women. An example of the strategies in place include the issue of gender alerts, in which local authorities must implement immediate measures to protect women's physical safety and rights and to thoroughly investigate complaints. However, only about 15 percent of women in Mexico are now covered by these gender alerts, and the implementation of the program has not shown a marked reduction in violence against women. Many states have justice centers where women can receive medical and psychological care and legal help.

Personal Well-Being

Mexico has implemented a number of policies and initiatives to improve the well-being of its citizens, to varying degrees of success. Many of these areas remain in flux.

In 2011, the people of Cherán fought back against violence and corruption. They fought criminal networks and took their village back but lost some of their own in the process. Each year, villagers march on the anniversary to remember those they lost in the conflict.

Education

In Mexico, almost 95 percent of the population age 15 and older is literate (able to read and write), and the average number of years an individual attends school rose from 13 years in 2014 to almost 15 years in 2017. Enrollment itself has improved since the start of the twenty-first century; even though Mexico's level of educational attainment remains low compared to other developed nations, enrollment increased from 42 percent to 53 percent in 2012. Graduation rates improved by 14 percentage points during that same time frame.

Full-time education is mandatory for all children ages four to 15, thanks to government reforms implemented in recent years. The government's goal is to have all Mexican children attending school full time by the year 2022, via the Full-Time Schools Program. Increases in secondary graduation rates are another major goal of educational reform programs, because only 37 percent of adults reported having graduated from secondary school in 2017.

Primary education, which includes first grade through sixth grade, became compulsory in 2009. Because the Secretariat of Public Education determines that primary school is essential to the attainment of basic

A group of schoolchildren sit in their classroom.

education, it is free of charge and includes a mandated year of preschool. The curriculum is standardized for both public and private schools and includes Spanish, natural sciences, history and geography, mathematics, art, and physical education.

Following the completion of primary school, Mexican students move on to what is referred to as lower secondary education, which covers seventh through ninth grades. It is free at state schools. Lower secondary students choose either an academic track or a technical track. The technical track provides students with nonacademic programming that emphasizes **vocational**, artistic, or commercial training.

Students in the academic track typically continue their education at the upper secondary level, which covers 10th through 12th grades. Admission to upper secondary education varies by institution, and many hold affiliations with public universities. Other upper secondary schools may be state-controlled, private, or preparatory schools. At this level, students again choose between two programming tracks: academic university preparatory or professional technical education. The academic track begins with two years of a general curriculum before a final year of specialized study, and the professional track provides technical preparation for students who plan to enter the workforce immediately after graduation. Many professional technical institutions offer vocational education as well.

Two students set up a robot prototype in their postgraduate technical classroom.

The Discontent of Mexican Teachers

In 2013, Mexican President Enrique Peña Nieto introduced a sweeping educational reform program meant to change the educational system, improve curriculum and learning standards, end corruption, and reduce the power of the nation's teachers' union: an ambitious goal for a country that ranks last in education among the 35 countries that are part of the Organization for Economic Cooperation and Development (OECD). This goal was undermined by two 2017 reports that the ministry in charge of the reforms spent almost 2,700 percent more on public relations than budgeted, yet teacher training programs went unfunded and schools were left without roofs, electricity, or running water.

Mexico's teachers have continually resisted the implementation of the controversial reforms that called for the closing of schools in favor of potential privatization, attacks on union rights, and rigid teacher evaluations that make it easier to fire them. Resistance to the reforms has resulted in the arrest of dissenting union officials and a 2016 instance of a police shooting that left at least eight protesters dead.

In the southern state of Oaxaca, teachers have formed La CNTE (or the National Coordinating Committee of Education Workers, as the name translates to in English). Among their efforts to resist the reforms, members of La CNTE have marched in Mexico City to protest the support their parent union has given to the reforms. They have also refused to take the national examinations the government now requires for teacher certification on the grounds that the test does nothing to evaluate performance in the classroom or account for local conditions in schools.

In addition, La CNTE has developed and offered its own plan to change education in Oaxaca. It calls for more teacher training alongside the involvement of parents in the classroom and school communities. Its plan stems from a desire to improve working conditions for its members and learning conditions for its students in the face of budget cuts, school closings and consolidations, class sizes that can number up to 60 students, and the refusal by school officials to replace retired teachers.

Information Access

Mexico has had laws regarding access to information since 2002, and in 2015, the National Congress passed the General Transparency Law to demand uniform access to information. This legislation was cited as key to fighting corruption, improving the rule of law, and bringing about economic growth. The implementation of this law has varied between municipalities due to each state's capabilities and political willpower.

Overall, Mexico's Freedom of Information Act was improved in that citizens' requests for information now receive a response; however, the rate at which requests are handled lags behind international standards. The government began a public-private partnership with broadband providers in 2017, with the intention of increasing access and usage across the country; however, many in rural areas still do not have reliable Internet access. Concerns arose through 2017 and 2018 about the government's use of spyware to track Internet use by journalists. Additionally, 42 journalists died in high-profile, violent killings in 2017, purportedly due to their work in reporting on government corruption and organized crime.

Health and Wellness

Mexico has experienced improvements in health and wellness over the past several years, and the gains are most evident in a 17-year improvement to the average life expectancy. In 2017, Mexicans lived, on average, to be 76 years old (the average life expectancy for men was about 73 years of age, whereas women on average lived to be 79 years of age). Much of this is due to better access to health care and initiatives designed to educate the public on nutritional choices, as well as preventative medicine.

Although Internet access isn't available all across the country, certain territories are working to make it easier. Pictured here, a tourist accesses the Internet in a local park in Merida.

In 2009, there was a swine flu outbreak. Many people wore masks to prevent germs from spreading.

Health concerns that face Mexico include infectious diseases like **dengue fever** and waterborne illnesses like hepatitis A. Less than a percent (0.3 percent) of adults have been diagnosed with HIV/AIDS, which equals about 230,000 cases reported in 2017.

Outbreaks of the Zika virus have caused concern for many. This mosquito-borne virus is usually harmless to adults but can be very dangerous for pregnant women. The virus causes fever or rash and can cause a condition called microcephaly—which causes abnormal brain development—in an unborn baby. The rate of babies born with microcephaly rose from 3.7 in 100,000 births to 11.7 in 100,000 births after the introduction of the Zika virus. Poor households are most at risk of exposure to Zika and tend to have the fewest resources to handle its effects.

Environment

Mexico faces environmental problems stemming from its manufacturing sectors and practices of deforestation. Air pollution has reached such a high level that many of the country's urban areas are continually blanketed by smog caused by industrial and vehicular emissions. This leads to a range of health problems, including asthma, cardiovascular diseases, and lung cancer, particularly among children and the elderly.

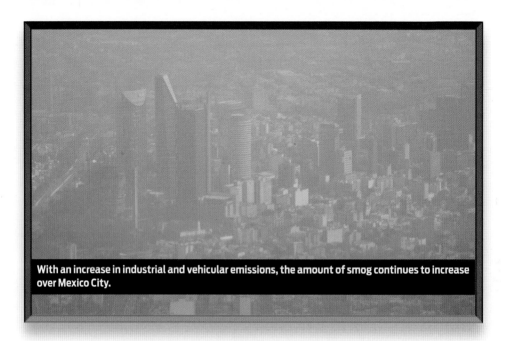

With an increase in industrial and vehicular emissions, the amount of smog continues to increase over Mexico City.

Clean water, or the lack thereof, is another issue for Mexico. Waste runoff from industrial sites and the effects of human usage have decreased the quality of Mexico's water supply to the point that Mexicans typically consume bottled water at a much higher rate than they do tap water.

Deforestation poses another problem, because people clear land for agricultural use and housing. Between 2000 and 2005, Mexico lost about 7 percent of its forest cover. Deforestation also contributes to climate change.

Mexico's government has committed to reducing its carbon emissions, both by becoming party to the Paris Climate Agreement as well as passing its General Law on Climate Change. This law aims to lower greenhouse gas emissions by 30 percent by the year 2020 and by 50 percent by the year 2050.

Opportunity

Improvement of personal opportunity is an area the Mexican government has promoted in recent years, especially in terms of access to education. Many people report having high levels of civic engagement.

Personal and Political Rights

Under the Constitution, Mexicans are guaranteed a number of personal freedoms and rights, including freedom of speech and the right to vote. Mexicans generally report a high level of civic engagement, and the government has increasingly used the Internet to build participation in

government and make access to public services and information a simple process.

Despite these efforts, corruption exists at high levels of government and has for a number of years. Activists and journalists fell victim to attempts by the government to spy on their electronic communications in 2017, and some journalists have been targeted and killed for published criticisms. A number of deficits in the rule of law prevent citizens from fully exercising their rights, and both state and non-state entities have been accused of human rights abuses by the international community. Corrupt officials seem to act with impunity, and speculation has arisen that the 2018 election may not have been completely fair and free.

Freedom of Choice

Cultural and religious traditions hold a good deal of sway in Mexico when considering people's freedom of choice to engage in certain social and economic activities. As a democracy with a growing economy, people generally have free access to consumer products and services. Most Mexicans feel they have choice and control over their lives. It is typically in the arena of societal norms that Mexicans may find their freedom to choose somewhat limited.

Almost 67 percent of women reported having access to contraception in 2018, and birth control is available over the counter. However, despite the availability of contraception, education in its proper usage is lacking, and many people do not use it effectively.

A historic trend of government programs and the health-care system failing to meet the needs of mothers and families created an extremely high instance of abortions in the late 2000s. A 2009 report from three higher-education institutes (the Instituto Nacional de Estadística y Geografía [INEGI], El Colegio de México, and the Guttmacher Institute) estimated that for every 15 births, 12 abortions were performed. Though not illegal, abortion is highly restricted in Mexico and yet widely practiced. Planned Parenthood estimates that between 500,000 and 1.5 million abortions are illegally performed in Mexico each year by unlicensed practitioners; of those, 150,000 women must be treated at local hospitals for complications.

Tolerance and Inclusion

Social inclusion and tolerance have been identified by Mexican leaders, including former president Enrique Peña Nieto, as being key values in Mexican society. For a country with a diverse population, this statement is important.

But a recent study out of the National Institute of Geography and Statistics points out that, although Mexican society includes an incredible range of racial skin tones and prides itself on its tolerance and inclusion of all races, European influences from the colonial era linger in terms of how Mexicans of different races view each other. Institutionalized racism exists and is evident when examining the educational attainment of dark-skinned versus lighter-skinned Mexicans.

Many business leaders in Mexico, as well as educational institutions, have begun to promote the open inclusion of LGBTQ community members. This comes in the form of nondiscrimination policies, employee resource groups or diversity and inclusion councils, and engagement in public activities in support of LGBTQ inclusion.

Higher Education

The higher-education system in Mexico operates similarly to the model used in the United States. Tertiary education students may attend public universities, technological institutions, teacher-training institutes, or private institutions. Each Mexican state has both a teacher-training college and a public university.

Undergraduate programs may last anywhere from two to six years, depending on the degree program. Associate degree programs are typically shortened to two years in length, and these degrees can be applied to further higher education. Some programs, such as those for accounting, engineering, law, and architecture, are five-year programs. Students can also complete graduate-level work to obtain a master's or doctoral degree, or attend a one-year program to obtain a specialist license.

Many of Mexico's universities have been rated as top institutions in Latin America, with 65 of them appearing on the 2018 ranking of top universities from QS World University Rankings for Latin America. The three highest-rated universities are Universidad Nacional Autómoma de México (UNAM) based in Mexico City, Tecnológico de Monterrey, and Instituto Politécnico National (IPN), also near Mexico City. Other major universities include the following:

- Universidad Iberoamericana

- Universidad Anahuac

- Instituto Tecnológico Autonomo de México

- Universidad Autómoma Metropolitana

- Universidad Autómoma de Nuevo León

- Benemérita Universidad Autómoma de Puebla

Enrollment in Mexico's universities has drastically increased in the past 30 years. In 1991, enrollment stood at about 15 percent of the population and by 2016 had risen to over 31 percent. These enrollment rates still lag behind other Latin American nations, but government reforms have been implemented since the 1980s to both manage as well as increase access to higher education while ensuring educational quality.

The on-campus library at Universidad Nacional Autónoma de México.

Text-Dependent Questions

1. Why have many Mexican teachers resisted government reforms of the education system?

2. What are Mexico's main environmental problems, and what steps has the government taken to address some of these issues?

3. What factors impact Mexican citizens' ability to exercise their political and civil rights?

Research Project

Choose a piece of legislation, which addresses crime rates and/or mandated responses to crimes, that has either been recently passed or is currently under debate in Mexico's National Congress. Research the effectiveness or projected effectiveness of the legislation. Write a four- to five-paragraph report from the viewpoint of a government advisor, outlining the reasons behind the legislation, the immediate effects of implementation, problems that have been identified, and suggested steps for improvement or continuation of effective implementation. Extension: Prepare a short visual presentation (PowerPoint, SlideShare, Google Slides) to present data surrounding this legislation.

Society and Culture

Mexico's vast diversity stems from generations of intermingling between Europeans, Africans, and the various native peoples who populated the region prior to the arrival of the Spanish conquistadors. Today, cultural influences from all of these groups can be found in multiple aspects of Mexican society, from religious traditions to cuisine and holiday celebrations.

Birth and Death Rates

Mexico's birth rate in 2017 stood at 18.3 births for every 1,000 people, a drop from the 2016 estimate of 19.02 births per 1,000 people. The average woman gives birth to just over two children in her lifetime. The birth rate has steadily declined over the past decade, resulting in an annual population growth rate that has dropped to less than a percent.

In the 1960s, average mothers gave birth to nearly seven children each. The consistent decrease in Mexico's birth rate began about 40 years ago. At that time, policies that focused on nation-building began to give way to a campaign aimed at increasing the availability and usage of contraceptive measures. Other social and economic factors, such as increased educational and career opportunities for women, as well as the higher price of housing, caused the size of Mexican families to shrink dramatically by 2010.

Words to Understand

Bilingual: The ability to speak two languages.

Geriatric: Of or relating to an elderly population.

Transatlantic slave trade: A segment of the global trade system that existed from the 1500s to the 1800s, involving the forced transport of tens of millions of African slaves across the Atlantic Ocean to the Americas.

A young girl plays with a coloring book. She is a part of the mestizo ethnic group—a mix between Spaniard and American Indian.

Mexico's Society and Culture at a Glance

Population	130,759,074 (2018)
Sex Ratio	0.96 male/female
Age Distribution	26.93 percent age 0–14; 17.54 percent age 15–24; 40.81 percent age 25–54; 7.64 percent age 55–64; 7.09 percent age 65 and over
Ethnic Groups	Amerindian-Spanish (mestizo) 62 percent, predominantly Amerindian 21 percent, Amerindian 7 percent, other, mostly European 10 percent
Religions	Roman Catholic 82.7 percent, Pentecostal 1.6 percent, Jehovah's Witness 1.4 percent; other Evangelical churches 5 percent, other 1.9 percent
Languages	Spanish only 92.7 percent, Spanish and indigenous languages 5.7 percent, indigenous only 0.8 percent, unspecified 0.8 percent

Newborn twins in Juárez, Mexico.

The overall decrease in the birth rate, and thus the slowdown in growth, may create social and economic issues down the road as the population ages. Estimates in the early 2010s indicate the expected number of citizens age 60 and over will rise from one in 10 to one in four. This would require an overhaul of the health-care system to better serve the needs of **geriatric** patients. Social security, too, could become strained as fewer young people are available to work in jobs that allow them to contribute to the nation's social security system.

The death rate, according to 2017 statistics, is 5.24 deaths for every 1,000 people, a rate that is comparable to regional neighbors Honduras and Venezuela, as well as the nations of Iran, Uzbekistan, and Samoa.

Population by Age

The average age of the Mexican population, according to 2017 estimates, is 28.3 years of age. Males have an average age of 27.2 years, whereas females have an average age of 29.4 years.

When breaking down the structure of the population into age-related segments, the largest demographic segment is people between the ages of 25 and 54 years, standing at approximately 41 percent. The next largest age group, at about 27 percent, is children from birth to age 14.

Mexicans between the ages of 15 and 24 years make up about 17.5 percent of the total population. Older adults from ages 55 to 64 (7.64 percent) and age 65 and up (7.09 percent) constitute the two smallest segments of the population.

Religions

Mexico has no official religion, but the dominant religion, by far, is Roman Catholicism. Almost 83 percent of Mexicans identified as Catholic in 2017, and many consider it an integral part of their identity and cultural heritage. Many festivals, activities, and holidays incorporate elements of the Catholic faith, and the display of religious idols and statuary is common in both private homes and public spaces.

Society tolerates other faiths, however, and the number of people who adhere to other Christian faiths is growing. Other faiths with significant numbers of adherents include Pentecostal Christians, various Evangelical Christians, and Jehovah's Witnesses. Many recent converts to these Protestant faiths were raised Catholic but converted due to disenchantment with the Catholic Church. There is also a very small percentage of Mexicans who practice Judaism or who do not adhere to any religious faith at all.

Revelers celebrate Saint Juan Diego—the first Roman Catholic indigenous saint from the Americas.

Traditional indigenous faiths and folk religions still exist to a small extent, often alongside traditional religions. Up to a third of Mexicans believe in magic and its influence over life events, especially for individuals who have not found reliable answers to their problems and fears in science and Catholicism. The belief in supernatural elements includes curses, witches, and the evil eye; healers and fortune-tellers are popular throughout Mexico. In some areas, indigenous traditions mix with Catholic beliefs, such as the creation of pseudo-saints that are believed to provide healing and protection and are worshipped with Catholic-like rituals.

Ethnic Groups

Although Mexico does not collect census data on ethnicity, identified ethnic groups include people who are mestizo, people who are predominantly Amerindian, and people who are fully Amerindian. Approximately 10 percent of Mexico's population identify as being part of other ethnic groups, most of which are of various European origins.

The largest ethnic group, mestizo, comprises 62 percent of the Mexican population. Mestizos embody the legacy of Spanish colonialism, because they are a mix of Spanish and Amerindian ancestry. For much of Mexico's modern history, mestizos have controlled most of the country's financial and governmental power.

Mexico's government recognizes over 50 indigenous groups, and 28 percent of the population identifies as being predominantly or completely Amerindian. The vast array of indigenous cultures survived due to their isolation in rural areas of the country, and people of Amerindian ethnicity have been able to retain a strong sense of identity, including customs and rituals that have survived for centuries. Members of Amerindian groups, however, are more likely to face conditions of poverty. The largest Amerindian group is the Nahua, who are descended from the Aztecs.

Although Mexico has long celebrated its mixed-race heritage, studies from the early to mid-2010s have revealed a trend in which the native population of Mexico faces discrimination and segregation, forced by circumstance to live in marginalized communities of the nation's capital. Colonial policies created economically depressed rural areas where native populations were forced to live, and as people from these rural areas began migrating into urban centers, including Mexico City, they faced further economic and social segregation. Viewed as outsiders with no territory, many created informal settlements or squatted in derelict parts of the city center, relying on social welfare and earning inconsistent incomes as hawkers or in domestic service. Institutional polices for integrating the indigenous population have existed for almost a hundred years, but the

A man from the mestizo ethnic group in traditional clothing.

Members of the Nahua group.

ambiguous nature of these policies proved them ineffective without social and cultural supports.

Languages

Spanish is the official language of Mexico and is the only language spoken by almost 93 percent of the population. A little less than 6 percent of the population speak both Spanish and an indigenous language, while less than 1 percent speak only indigenous languages.

Over 140 indigenous languages are found in Mexico. Nahuatl, the language of the Nahua (Mexico's largest indigenous group), was spoken by at least 1.7 million people in 2005. The next largest indigenous language group is Maya, with about a million speakers. Other indigenous languages include Zapotec (about 500,000 speakers), Mixtec (about 260,000 speakers), and Purepechas (about 130,000 speakers).

The number of indigenous language speakers has dwindled dramatically in certain areas, and in 2014, Mexico's Center of Research and Higher Studies in Social Anthropology (CIESAS) identified 60 native Mexican languages at risk of vanishing. Twenty-one of these languages were, at the time, spoken by only a handful of elderly persons, making them critically endangered languages. CIESAS cites migration to urban centers, pressures to learn

Ethnic and Racial Discrimination in Mexico

A 2017 study by the Latin American Public Opinion Project at Vanderbilt University (LAPOP) revealed another facet of segregation and discrimination in Mexico: the effect of racism, based on facial skin tone, educational attainment, and economic mobility. LAPOP created an 11-point standardized scale to categorize the skin tone of the university's Americas Barometer, then surveyed individuals in 34 countries in North, Central, and South America and the Caribbean. Respondents provided information about education and wealth, and LAPOP researchers examined the data for correlations with race.

The results showed that white-skinned Mexicans tended to complete more years of schooling than Mexicans with the darkest skin tones on the scale, with average years of education standing at 10 years to 6.5 years respectively—a 45 percent gap in educational attainment. Similar correlations were found in terms of wealth, using the average Mexican household income (in U.S. dollars) of $193 per month. People with lighter skin reported monthly household incomes at $220 a month, compared to $137 per month for those with darker skin. Additional information about material wealth revealed that darker-skinned Mexicans were more likely to lack running water or in-home bathrooms.

Respondents to the poll did not believe skin color created a source of prejudice in their lives, citing gender and social class as having a greater impact. The results of LAPOP's study show, however, that race does impact educational development and the accumulation of wealth more than other demographic variables, including the urban-rural divide and regional differences. LAPOP has already determined that its future research will examine the factors that create these racial inequalities and other areas of impact, like access to health care and employment opportunities, with the end goal of providing lawmakers the information needed to design policies that can reduce racial inequality.

and use Spanish over indigenous languages in school and the workplace, and economic and social factors as reasons for the decline.

In an effort to save indigenous languages, researchers and linguists began working to create digital resources intended to preserve what are termed *heritage languages*. Efforts to boost interest in younger generations include a push for **bilingual** education in regional schools and the leveraging of communication technology tools like smartphones and language-specific buttons on cell phone and computer keypads.

An indigenous woman carries her child on her back. She is a part of the Huichol tribe.

Foods

Mexican cuisine is a mix of the various cultures found within its history, from native indigenous groups to African influences brought during the **transatlantic slave trade**. Many traditional dishes incorporate ingredients that are native to the region and were used by the Aztecs, Mayans, and Zapotec before Europeans arrived. Traditional ingredients include corn or maize, beans, tomatoes, peppers, sweet potatoes, squash, and various herbs. The arrival of Europeans introduced livestock like cattle, pigs, and chickens, and later plants of Asian origin like sugarcane and wheat. Other basic staples of Mexican cuisine include the following:

- Tortillas, traditionally made of corn but also from flour, and served alongside meals in the place of bread or incorporated into many dishes such as enchiladas or quesadillas

- Frijoles, or beans, which are commonly boiled and then fried, then served as a main ingredient or a side dish

- Chilies, ranging from small and hot to large and mild, used for main dishes, such as the large poblano peppers stuffed with meat or cheese to make *chiles rellenos*, or as a garnish

- Guacamole, a dip or garnish made from mashed avocadoes mixed with onions, chilies, and cilantro

A woman sells maize dough at a market. The dough is then used to make tortillas for enchiladas, tacos, or quesadillas.

Chiles rellenos are made with large poblano peppers.

Various sauces and salsas are used to add spice and flavor to Mexican dishes.

- Salsa, literally "sauce," made from a mix of tomatoes, onions, chilies, and cilantro, with varying levels of spiciness

- Enchiladas, made with tortillas coated in a tomato and chili sauce and stuffed with beans, pork, chicken, or beef, then folded and baked

- Quesadillas, made with tortillas stuffed with cheese and either grilled or fried

- Mole sauce, made from chilies, spices, and chocolate, often served over chicken

- Tacos, made with corn tortillas that are fried until crispy and then stuffed with meat and other fillings

Breakfast in Mexico is simple, usually just coffee and sweet rolls (*pan dulce*). Eggs may be included, as in dishes like *huevos rancheros*, where eggs are fried and served with tortillas and beans. Mexicans eat lunch between one and three o'clock in the afternoon. It may consist of a soup and a main dish that includes meat, as well as rice, tortillas, coffee, and a dessert. It is typically the largest meal of the day. Supper, a light evening meal, may be served at nine o'clock or later, but in urban areas may be replaced by an elaborate dinner. Traditional foods are often an integral part of many holidays and family celebrations.

Mole sauce served over chicken.

Local women prepare tortillas in a bakery.

A Sweet Treat

Chocolate, today enjoyed worldwide (often in the form of candy), is native to Mexico and was originally consumed as a hot drink flavored with dried chili powder and considered a beverage fit only for royalty.

National Holidays

Holidays in Mexico range from cultural and religious celebrations to civic holidays marking important events throughout the year. Though celebrations vary by holiday and region, typical aspects found nationwide include music, parades, fireworks, and food.

Because Mexico is a predominantly Catholic country, religious observances are a major part of Mexican culture and heritage. Many Catholic feast days, which mark either the births or deaths of saints, are observed throughout the year. Major religious holidays and observances include those that surround the Christmas and Easter seasons.

Religious Holidays

Observance of Christmas begins on December 16th with the celebration of Las Posadas. During the nine days between December 16th and 24th, children portray the story of the Holy Family coming to Bethlehem in search of shelter. The children, dressed in silver or gold robes and carrying candles and images of saints Mary and Joseph, travel door-to-door in their neighborhoods, asking each neighbor if they have lodging for the Holy Family. Adults follow the children's procession, playing music along the way. At each stop, tradition holds that the homeowners refuse the request for lodging but often provide refreshments. Christmas carols are sung and passages from the Bible are read at each stop as well. At the end of the procession, Mass is held, followed by a celebration in which children break open piñatas full of candy, toys, and coins.

Another important celebration that is part of the Christmas season is Día de los Santos Reyes, or Three Kings Day, on January 6th. This date is also known as the Epiphany in many other Catholic cultures. Families traditionally exchange gifts on Día de los Santos Reyes, rather than on Christmas Day, though traditions from the United States and Northern Europe, including the exchange of gifts on Christmas Day, are gaining popularity in Mexico.

The people of Tlaxcala light flares and sparklers during the Christmas celebration.

Piñatas on display at a market in preparation for Christmas celebrations.

Just before Las Posadas, Mexicans observe Día de Nuestra Señora de Guadalupe on December 12th, honoring Our Lady of Guadalupe, the patron saint of Mexico. This feast day commemorates the appearance of the dark-skinned Virgin Mary who appeared to a poor Indian convert to Catholicism in 1531. Mexicans hold parades and religious celebrations during this holiday.

Lent, a solemn season that lasts for 40 days before Easter, varies on the calendar but usually begins in mid- to late February and ends anywhere from the end of March through mid-April. The pre-Lenten celebration of Carnaval mirrors traditional Mardi Gras celebrations held in the United States and includes parades and lively street parties. Holy Week, or Semana Santa, marks the end of Lent with festivals and parades on Good Friday and Easter Sunday. Many Mexicans take family vacations to the beaches or mountains during Semana Santa.

One of the most well-known holidays in Mexico is Día de los Muertos, or Day of the Dead. This holiday begins on October 31st and ends on November 2nd each year, and each region celebrates with its own cultural variations. This holiday mixes solemnity with celebration, because it is a time when Mexicans honor and remember members of their families who

have passed away. People set up family altars or public displays, known as *ofrendas,* decorated with photographs, mementos, and offerings of food, refreshments, and symbolic gifts. In some regions of Mexico, the observance may include vigils and feasts in cemeteries or the creation and consumption of candy skeletons or a sweet bread called *pan de muerto.*

Revelers celebrate Day of the Dead with a parade.

Learn more about Día de los Muertos.

Civic Holidays

Observances of civic and national holidays in Mexico surround the commemoration of major historical or governmental moments throughout history. These holidays may include parades and other public celebrations, and many also result in a day off from work and the closure of banks and government offices. Some of these holidays include Constitution Day on February 5th, the memorial of Benito Juárez's birthday on March 21st, Labor Day on May 1st, and Revolution Day on November 20th (these holidays may be observed on the Monday prior to the holiday itself).

Mexicans celebrate their independence on September 16th. Officially called Día de la Independencia, this holiday is also referred to as Diez y Seis (Spanish for 16). Banks, schools, government offices, and businesses close, and large parties and parades are held in many major cities. Public areas are often decorated with flags, flowers, and other decorations in red, green, and white—the colors of the Mexican flag. On the evening of September 15th, town and city mayors often read the *grito*, or cry to revolution, delivered by mestizo priest Father Hidalgo y Costilla in 1810, which spurred Mexicans to fight against the Spanish-born ruling class of the colony of New Spain.

Cinco de Mayo is celebrated on May 5th. Schools and government offices close, and the states of Puebla and Veracruz hold a regional holiday. Although Cinco de Mayo has become a major celebration for Mexican-Americans in the United States, it is not widely observed in Mexico outside of Puebla. The holiday commemorates an early victory over French invasion forces in the Battle of Puebla on May 5, 1862. Though the battle did not rid Mexico of the presence of French forces, the Mexican victory boosted the confidence of the army and the Mexican people and bolstered national unity. In Puebla, people celebrate by holding parades and battle reenactments. Reenactments are also held in other parts of Mexico, including a rock formation in Mexico City called Peñón de los Baños, located near neighborhoods where former residents of Puebla now reside.

Text-Dependent Questions

1. What problems could Mexico face in the coming decades due to its declining birth rate?

2. How has religion, specifically Catholicism, influenced Mexican cultural traditions?

3. Why are researchers and linguists developing online databases and technology tools to help preserve indigenous languages in Mexico?

Research Project

Look into LAPOP's research into the effects of racism on Mexican society. Write a five- to six-paragraph essay outlining the main findings, examining the reported perceptions of participants, and evaluating the claims made by LAPOP regarding its poll results. Extension: Create a PowerPoint slideshow to present your learning and analysis to your peers.

Cinco de Mayo is a regional holiday, celebrated only in the states of Puebla and Veracruz.

Series Glossary of Key Terms

Absolute monarchy: A form of government led by a single individual, usually called a king or a queen, who has control over all aspects of government and whose authority cannot be challenged.

Amendment: A change to a nation's constitution or political process, sometimes major and sometimes minor.

Arable: Describing land that is capable of being used for agriculture.

Asylum: When a nation grants protection to a refugee or immigrant who has been persecuted in his or her own country.

Austerity: Governmental policies that include spending cuts, tax increases, or a combination of the two, with the aim of reducing budget deficits.

Authoritarianism: Governmental structure in which all citizens must follow the commands of the reigning authority, with few or no rights of their own.

Autocracy: Ruling regime in which the leader has absolute power.

Bicameral: A legislative body structured into two branches or chambers.

Bilateral: Something that involves two nations or parties.

Bloc: A group of countries or parties with similar aims and purposes.

Cash crop: Agriculture meant to be sold directly for profit rather than consumed.

Central bank: A government-authorized bank whose purpose is to provide money to retail, commercial, investment, and other banks.

Cleric: A general term for a religious leader such as a priest or imam.

Coalition force: A force made up of military elements from nations that have created a temporary alliance for a specific purpose.

Colonization: The process of occupying land and controlling a native population.

Commodities: Raw products of agriculture or mining, such as corn or precious metals, that can be bought and sold on the market.

Communism: An economic and political system where all property is held in common; a form of government in which a one-party state controls the means of production and distribution of resources.

Conscription: Compulsory enlistment into state service, usually the military.

Constituency: A body of voters in a specific area who elect a representative to a legislative body.

Constitution: A written document or unwritten set of traditions that outline the powers, responsibilities, and limitations of a government.

Coup: A quick change in government leadership without a legal basis, most often by violent means.

De-escalation: Reduction or elimination of armed hostilities in a war zone, often directed by a cease-fire or truce.

Defector: A citizen who flees his or her country, often out of fear of oppression or punishment, to start a life in another country.

Demilitarized zone: An area where military personnel, installations, and related activities are prohibited.

Depose: The act of removing a head of government through force, intimidation, and/or manipulation.

Détente: An easing of hostility or strained relations, particularly between countries.

Developing nation: A nation that does not have the social or physical infrastructure necessary to provide a modern standard of living to its middle- and working-class population.

Diaspora: The members of a community that spread out into the wider world, sometimes assimilating to new cultures and sometimes retaining most or all of their original culture.

Diktat: An order from an authority given without popular approval.

Disenfranchise: To take away someone's rights.

Displaced persons: Persons who are forced to leave their home country or a region of their country due to war, persecution, or natural disasters.

Economic boom: A period of rapid economic and financial growth, resulting in greater wealth and more purchasing power.

Economic reserves: Currency, usually in the form of gold, used to support the paper money distributed through an economy, available to be used by a government when its own currency does not have enough value.

Edict: A proclamation by a person in authority that functions the same as a law.

Embargo: An official ban on trade.

Federation: A country formed by separate states with a central government that manages national and international affairs, but control over local matters is retained by individual states.

Food insecurity: Being without reliable access to nutritious food at an affordable price and in sufficient quantity.

Free-floating currency: A currency whose value is determined by the free market, changing according to supply and demand for that currency.

Fundamentalist: A political and/or religious ideology based explicitly on traditional orthodox concepts, with rejection of modern values.

Gross Domestic Product (GDP): The total value of goods and services a country produces in a given time frame.

Hegemony: Dominance of one nation over others.

Heretical: When someone's beliefs contradict an orthodox religion.

Indigenous: Referring to a person or group native to a particular place.

Industrialization: The transition from an agricultural economy to a manufacturing economy.

Inflation: A general increase in prices and a decrease in the purchasing value of money.

Insurgency: An organized movement aimed at overthrowing or destroying a government.

Islamist: A military or political organization that believes in the fundamentals of Islam as the guiding principle, rather than secular law; often used synonymously (although not always accurately) with Islamic terrorism.

Jihad: A struggle or exertion on behalf of Islam, sometimes through armed conflict.

Judiciary: A network of courts within a society and their relationship to each other.

Mercantilism: A historical economic theory that focuses on the trade of raw materials from a colony to the mother country, and of manufactured goods from the mother country to the colony, for the profit of the mother country.

Migrant: A person who moves from place to place, either by choice or due to warfare or other economic, political, or environmental crises.

Militia: A group of volunteer soldiers who do not fight with a military full-time.

Municipal elections: Elections held for office on the local level, such as town, city, or county.

Nationalize: When an industry or sector of the economy is totally owned and operated by the government.

Parliamentary: Governmental structure in which executive power is awarded to a cabinet of legislative body members, rather than elected by the people directly.

Paramilitary: Semimilitarized force, trained in tactics and organized by rank, but not officially part of a nation's formal military.

Patriarchy: A system of society or government in which power is held by men.

Police state: Nation in which the state closely monitors activity and harshly punishes any citizen thought to be critical of society or the government.

Populism: An approach to politics, often with authoritarian elements, that emphasizes the role of ordinary people in a society's government over that of an elite class.

Propagandist: A person who disseminates government-created communications, like TV shows and posters, that seek to directly influence and control a national audience to serve the needs of the government, sometimes employing outright falsehoods.

Proportional representation: An electoral system in which political parties gain seats in proportion to the number of votes cast for those seats.

Protectionist: Actions on behalf of a government to stem international trade in favor of helping domestic businesses and producers.

Reactionary: A person who opposes new social and economic ideas or reforms; a person who seeks a return to past forms of governance.

Referendum: A decision on a particular issue put up to a popular vote.

Refugee: A person who leaves his or her home nation, by force or by choice, to flee from war or oppression.

Reparations: Payments made to someone to make amends for wrongdoing.

Republicanism: A political philosophy of representative government in which citizens elect leaders to govern.

Rubber-stamp legislature: Legislative body with formal authority but little, if any, decision-making power and subordinate to another branch of government or political party leadership.

Sanctions: Political and/or economic punishments levied against another nation as punishment for wrongdoing.

Secretariat: A permanent administrative office or department, usually in government, and the staff of that office or department.

Sect: A subgroup of a major religion, with individual beliefs or philosophies that divide it from other subgroups of the religion.

Sovereignty: The ability of a country to rule itself.

Statute: A law created and passed by a legislative body.

Subsidies: Amounts of money that a government gives to a particular industry to help manage prices or promote social or economic policies.

Tariff: A tax or fee placed on imported or exported products.

Theocratic: Of or relating to a theocracy, a form of government that lays claim to God as the source and justification of its authority.

Totalitarian: A form of government where power is in the hands of a single person or group.

Trade deficit: The degree to which a country must buy more imports than it sells exports; can reflect economic problems as well as strong buying power.

Trade surplus: The degree to which a country can sell more exports than it purchases; can reflect economic strength as well as poor buying power.

Welfare state: A system where the government publically funds programs to ensure the health and well-being of its citizens.

Chronology of Key Events

250–900 Classical Maya city-states flourish in the southern part of modern-day Mexico before a mysterious collapse.

900s Revitalized Maya civilization develops in the northern Yucatán peninsula, lasting until the sixteenth century.

1428 The Aztec Empire establishes control over much of central Mexico, lasting a century.

1519 Spanish conquistadors under Hernando Cortés land at Veracruz and claim the land for Spain.

1521 Cortés allies with native anti-Aztec forces and captures Tenochtitlan (modern-day Mexico City).

1521 Spain establishes the Viceroyalty of New Spain.

1810 Father Hidalgo y Costilla issues his "Cry of Dolores" calling for mestizo revolutionaries to revolt against the Spanish-born ruling class of New Spain.

1821 Spain recognizes Mexico's independence; the Mexican Empire is created from the southwestern United States to the southern border of modern-day Costa Rica.

1824 Mexico becomes a federal republic; the southern provinces secede to become Costa Rica, Guatemala, Honduras, El Salvador, and Nicaragua.

1836 Texas enters a war for independence from Mexico and secedes; it will later be annexed by the United States.

1846 Mexico goes to war with the United States.

1848 Mexican-American War ends, with Mexico forced to sell its northern provinces to the United States; this territory becomes the modern states of California, Nevada, New Mexico, Arizona, and Utah.

1855 A period of liberal reforms begins, limiting the power and landholdings of the Catholic Church.

1862 The Mexican army defeats invading French forces at the Battle of Puebla, unifying the country against France.

1864 Archduke Maximilian of Austria is made emperor of Mexico by the French and conservative landowners; he is executed by rebels three years later.

1867 The French are driven from Mexico.

1876 Porfirio Díaz takes over as dictator, bringing stability, modernization, and economic growth, but also political repression.

1910 The Mexican Revolution begins.

1911 Díaz's dictatorship ends, but political unrest continues.

1913–14 Francisco Madero introduces land reform and labor legislation but is assassinated; Emiliano Zapata leads a peasant revolt in the south.

1916–17 The United States attempts an incursion against guerilla leader Francisco "Pancho" Villa.

1917 Mexican Constitution is ratified, establishing a constitutional government.

1920	Mexican Revolution officially ends; president Venustiano Carranza is assassinated, launching a decade of instability.
1929	Former president Plutarco Elias Calles forms the Institutional Revolutionary Party (PRI), which will dominate the government for 71 years.
1934	President Lazaro Cardenas begins a program to nationalize oil production, reform land laws, and expand industry.
1960	A decade of unrest and suppression begins as peasants and laborers demonstrate over unequal distribution of wealth.
1968	During a student demonstration at the Olympic Games in Mexico City, Mexican security forces fire on protesters, killing or wounding hundreds.
1976	Huge offshore oil reserves are discovered, becoming the mainstay of Mexico's oil production.
1985	A Mexico City earthquake kills thousands and leaves many more homeless.
1993	Mexico's National Congress ratifies NAFTA.
1994	Government troops brutally suppress the guerilla rebellion by the Zapatista National Liberation Army; greater autonomy for indigenous Mayans in Chiapas state is agreed upon by the government and Zapatistas.
1996	Southern insurgency escalates as the Popular Revolutionary Army attacks government troops.
1997	The PRI loses its majority in the Chamber of Deputies for the first time since 1929.
2000	Vincete Fox becomes the first opposition candidate to win the presidential election.
2002	Secret security files on political activists from the 1960s and 1970s are released, revealing the repression of activists by the government.
2006	Conservative candidate Felipe Calderon wins the presidential election; a new federal police force is created to tackle the problem of drug cartels.
2009	Open warfare between rival drug gangs erupts on the border with the United States; Mexican army troops enter Ciudad Juárez.
2012	The army arrests the leader of a drug cartel accused of killing and mutilating 49 people, one of the worst atrocities committed in the ongoing drug cartel war.
2012	Enrique Peña Nieto wins the presidency, putting the PRI back in power.
2013	Miguel Angel Trevino Morales, head of the Zetas drug cartel, is arrested under president Peña Nieto's policy of targeting local cartel bosses.
2014	Congress approves reforms to the energy sector to open the market to foreign oil firms.
2018	Andrés Manuel López Obrador wins the presidential election, ushering in the political domination of populists in Mexico.

Further Reading & Internet Resources

Books

Cassriel, Betsy, and Ricardo Mora. *My Teenage Life in Mexico (Customs and Cultures of the World)*. Broomall, PA: Mason Crest, 2017. Information about Mexico's history, economy, culture, and politics are presented through the voice of a Mexican teenager.

Foster, Lynn V. *A Brief History of Mexico*. New York: Checkmark Books, 2009. A look at Mexico's history from the pre-Columbian era to the late 2000s, including discussion of such issues as the war on drug cartels, corruption, multiparty democracy, and NAFTA.

Ganster, Paul, and David E Lorey. *The U.S.–Mexico Border Today: Conflict and Cooperation in Historical Perspectives* (Latin American Silhouettes). Lanham, MD: Rowman & Littlefield Publishers, 2015. A comprehensive look at the historical development of current politics and key issues surrounding the border region between the United States and Mexico.

Gitlin, Marty. *The Border Wall with Mexico (Current Controversies)*. Farmington Hills, MI: Greenhaven Press, 2017. A collection of articles from diverse viewpoints that examine the issue of a border wall between the United States and Mexico.

Haugen, David M. *Mexico (Opposing Viewpoints)*. Farmington Hills, MI: Greenhaven Press, 2011. A collection of essays on various issues facing Mexico in the late 2000s and early 2010s, including economic, social, and political instability, foreign relations with the United States, and internal problems like the war on drug cartels. Topics are discussed through points and counterpoints to present varied perspectives of the issues.

Web Sites

Mexico. *Country Profile. BBC News. https://www.bbc.com/news/world-latin-america-18095241. An online country profile with information about the government, economy, and history and links to current news stories about Mexico.*

Mexico. *Encyclopedia Britannica. https://www.britannica.com/place/Mexico. An online encyclopedia entry with information about Mexico's geography, history, government, economy, society, and more.*

Mexico. *Population and Facts. The History Channel. https://www.history.com/topics/mexico. A topic overview page with links to information about Mexican regions, personalities, and historical events.*

Mexico Drug War Fast Facts. *CNN. https://www.cnn.com/2013/09/02/world/americas/mexico-drug-war-fast-facts/index.html. An overview, with timeline, of Mexico's ongoing war on drug cartels, with links to news articles.*

Nations Online. *Mexico. https://www.nationsonline.org/oneworld/mexico.htm. A comprehensive site with information about Mexico's culture, history, geography, and more, with links to multiple external Web sites.*

Index

Author's Biography

Jennifer L. Rowan teaches secondary social studies for Charlotte-Mecklenburg Schools in Charlotte, North Carolina. She holds two master's degrees, including a master of science in literacy education, and has over 12 years of teaching experience in New York and North Carolina. She is also a freelance writer and editor and an author of fiction. A native of upstate New York, near Syracuse, she now lives in the greater Charlotte area with her family.

Credits

Cover

Interior